# *Edinburgh in the '45*

# Edinburgh in the '45

*Bonnie Prince Charlie at Holyroodhouse*

## John Sibbald Gibson

Foreword by
the Rt Hon Norman Irons CBE
Lord Provost of the City of Edinburgh

Educated at Paisley Grammar School and Glasgow University, John Sibbald Gibson combined a career in the Scottish Office with a keen interest in eighteenth century Scotish history.

Other books he has written are
Ships of the '45;
Playing the Scottish Card: the Franco-Jacobite invasion of 1708;
The Jacobite Threat 1689-1759 (with Bruce Lenman);
Summer Hunting a Prince (with Alasdair Maclean);
The Thistle and the Crown; (the centenary history of the Scottish Office);
Deacon Brodie, Father to Jekyll and Hyde;
Lochiel of the '45: the Jacobite Chief and the Prince.

Cover illustration, Prince Charles Edward Stuart by Maurice Quentin de la Tour (Scottish National Portrait Gallery)

First published 1995 by The Saltire Society, 9 Fountain Close, High Street, Edinburgh EH1 1TF & Edinburgh District Council, Department of Recreation

The publishers acknowledge with thanks subsidy from the Scottish Arts Council towards the publication of this volume.

Printed and bound by Ritchie of Edinburgh.


A catalogue record for this book is available from the British Library.


ISBN 0 85411 067 4

# Contents

# *Acknowledgements*

This book arose out of discussion with the National Trust for Scotland.

My thanks are due to Lord Cameron, Professor David Daiches, Professor Bruce Lenman, Miss Iseabail Macleod, and to Dr Archie Turnbull, all of whom commented on my script; to Mr Iain MacIvor (late Principal Inspector of Ancient Monuments) for information about Holyrood as it was in 1745. I am grateful to the staff of the National Library of Scotland, the Edinburgh Central Library, and to the City Archivist. My thanks also to Ritchie of Edinburgh, printers, and to the City of Edinburgh District Council.

I must record my indebtedness to the Earl of Wemyss, Sir Donald Cameron of Lochiel, Drambuie Ltd, the Royal Bank of Scotland, and the Scottish National Portrait Gallery for permission to reproduce illustrations. All other illustrations are from the Edinburgh Room of the Edinburgh Central Library to whom a special word of thanks is due.

# *Foreword*

## *by the Rt. Hon. The Lord Provost, Norman Irons*

Bonnie Prince Charlie's court at Holyrood in 1745 was the last burst of sunlight on the Stuart Cause, and it was to make an indelible imprint on Edinburgh's history.

The Saltire Society are to be congratulated in giving us in *Edinburgh in the '45* what has not previously been attempted; a picture of the events of these autumn months as seen by those who were there at the time. So here are the excited words of a young lady come to town as she falls under the spell of the bonnie Prince; and the exasperated views of a nobleman in the Jacobite army as he becomes uneasily aware of the Prince's disastrous obstinacy. These contrast with the journal kept by a Grassmarket saddler who damns all Jacobites, and the account of a student volunteer for the defence of Edinburgh who witnessed the carnage of the battle of Prestonpans. In between are others who sit on the fence and watch. There are too the reports of the 'ambassador' from Louis XV of France who watches Charles Edward's desperate resolve to invade England and march straight for London. And all the while, towering above the city, there is Edinburgh Castle holding out for King George.

It has been said that of the tragedy of the 'Forty-Five was that it ever happened. But brave men died on both sides of the divide, and there were many who, in the words of Robert Burns, 'shook hands with ruin for what they esteemed their country's good'. So on this its 250th anniversary, the 'Forty-Five merits commemoration, particularly in Edinburgh, a commemoration which Edinburgh District Council are glad to support.

# The Background

By the early years of the eighteenth century the Royal House of Stuart had given Scotland her monarchs for 350 years, England for the previous hundred. The last Stuart monarch Anne, had also presided in 1707 over the union of Scotland with England into the unified realm of Great Britain. When Queen Anne died in 1714 the nearest in line to the throne was her half-brother James, exiled in France and debarred from the British throne by his adherence to the Catholic faith which his father King James II and VII had embraced. In preference to young James, Prince George of Hanover became King of Great Britain. But for many Scots, sentiment and religion induced strong feelings for the Stuarts who were still 'God's anointed'. Many yearned for an independent Scotland. In England too some felt that departure from the Stuarts' strict hereditary right to the throne was wrong. In 1715 the first Jacobite Rising broke out in Scotland. This and an associated rebellion in the north of England was defeated, as was a lesser Scottish rising with slender foreign support in 1719.

By 1745 a now elderly 'King James III' still lived in exile with his Jacobite Court in Rome. But his handsome twenty-five year old son, Charles Edward, was set on

*Edinburgh from the Lang Dykes*

1

winning back the British crown for the Stuarts. The European war of the 1740s ranging France against Britain seemed to offer him his opportunity. With some French help, he set sail from Nantes for Scotland in July 1745,

# I

# The Taking of Edinburgh

Like many a well-doing burgess before his day (and since) Patrick Crichton, a fifty-year-old saddler and ironmonger in Edinburgh's Grassmarket, had bought himself a country estate out of town: Woodhouselie, eight miles or so south of the Cross of Edinburgh, lying by the wooded banks of the River Esk. That momentous Sunday in the autumn of 1745 when the town prepared for attack by Prince Charles Edward Stuart's army of Highlanders, Crichton was at worship, not far from his home, in Glencorse Kirk when morning service was interrupted by a message from Edinburgh to a lady in the congregation. She was Mrs Philp, wife of the owner of the

nearby estate of Greenlaw who was also a director of the recently created Royal Bank of Scotland in Edinburgh; her husband warned that the Highland horde was now approaching the village of Corstorphine, four miles from town and only divided from Glencorse by the Pentlands ridge. A worried Mrs Philp left church in mid-sermon to join her husband in town. So did one of the elders, he to drive his master's horses to the seclusion of the hills. Patrick Crichton, too, itched to be away.

But this was the Scottish Sabbath, and from the pulpit of Glencorse Kirk the Reverend John Wilson bumbled on, Crichton recorded in his journal, 'with a long sermon and an ill-timed exhortation'. Able to stand it no longer, the Grassmarket saddler too left the church to climb with his sons over to the other side of the Pentlands. From there, laid out before him was the splendid panorama of Edinburgh and the Lothian plain, the waters of the Firth of Forth and the coast of Fife beyond. With his 'prospect'

*Map of Midlothian, 1735, by John Adair (excerpt)*

[telescope] he could just make out the scarlet and glitter of King George's dragoons drawn up 'at the west end of Corstorphine to the northwards of the highway where the two roads join'. Of the Highlanders there was nothing yet to be seen, but they could not be far off. The unbelievable was now about to happen.

It had been five weeks since Lord Provost Archibald Stewart and his Council had received a letter from the Marquis of Tweeddale, Secretary of State for Scotland at the court of King George II in distant London, warning that Charles Edward, 'the Pretender's eldest son', had embarked from the west of France. His purpose was thought to be to raise rebellion against King George II in the fond hope of winning the throne of Great Britain for his father, King James, in his Roman exile. Beyond deciding that the Town Guard be augmented by thirty, that the constables inquire if there were any suspicious characters about, and that innkeepers give the City Guard a list of strangers residing with them, the Council felt no alarm. But the following day Duncan Forbes, Lord President of the Court of Session and the keystone of King George's establishment in Scotland, learned from his Campbell friends in the west that Moidart was now aflame, since the Stuart Prince had now landed in the West Highlands, and was raising some sort of an army from the Jacobite clans who still held to their warlike traditions and their loyalty to the Stuarts. In his mind Duncan Forbes was half-prepared for this. Not three months past, Sir Hector Maclean, a land-less Jacobite but still the chief of the Macleans of Mull, had slipped into the port of Leith on a trading-smack from Boulogne with word for his leading Scottish support-ers from Charles Edward, then still in France. Forbes had had Sir Hector clapped into the custody of Edinburgh Castle from his lodgings in the Canongate; the identity of any newcomer could not long be kept secret in Edinburgh of the high lands and narrow wynds. But attempts by 'great Duncan' similarly to round up Scotland's two leading Jacobites, the Duke of Perth from his castle in Strathearn and Cameron of Lochiel in distant Lochaber had significantly failed. Something was in the wind.

'In his boots to go north' that August morning when the news from Moidart came in, Forbes had called on Lieutenant-General Sir John Cope, commander in chief of King George's forces in North Britain, 'a little dressy finical man' as the Scots saw him, to concert what was to be done. Forbes to hasten to his fine new house, Culloden near Inverness, from there to steady the uncertain loyalties of the clans. Sir John to assemble his guns and his 2000 infantry from their garrison and road-making duties, march with them up the military road from Stirling Castle, cross the Tay at Taybridge and on through the mountains to new-built Fort Augustus midway along the Great Glen. His two dragoon regiments to remain in the Lowlands, Gardiner's to guard the crossings of the River Forth above Stirling, Hamilton's to remain at Leith; Edinburgh Castle to be provisioned and the invalid company garrisoned there to be reinforced with two companies of Lascelles Foot. In 1719 the same timely strategy of hastening government troops to the hills to confront Jacobite rebels had triumphed. Forbes was confident that this latest rising in the West Highlands would likewise be, as he put it, 'a fire of straw', soon smothered.

For the rest of that August, Edinburgh had been in the dark about the progress of Sir John and his red-coated army. With Stuart supporters in the north seeing to it that the weekly post from Inverness was stopped, the town was just as ignorant of the progress of Charles Edward's mad-cap adventurism.

*Duncan Forbes, Lord President, attributed to Jeremiah Davison (Scottish National Portrait Gallery).*

Towards the end of the month the Lord Provost had convened a public meeting in the New Church, one of the four parts into which old St Giles was divided, to consider what was to be done in the unlikely event of the town having to defend herself. There was talk of repairing the city walls, now dilapidated in parts and at the best more akin to high park walls than modern fortification; also of raising a regiment of foot at the town's expense. But here was difficulty. Statute law from the troubled times of King Charles II expressly forbade the raising of troops other than by the King's authority. Nothing for it but that the Lord Advocate, the government's senior law officer in Scotland, should send a messenger to London with all speed to seek King George's permission. And so a week was lost.

On the last day of August, there came disturbing news from Perthshire. Sir John's army, this said, had failed to confront the rebels, was now at Fort St. George, the recently strengthened castle overlooking the River Ness and the burgh of Inverness; and the Stuart Prince with a Highland army was already in the Braes of Athole. Four days later came the thunderclap: the Highlanders had seized Perth, by road only sixty miles away. But that day there also came to Edinburgh Castle an emissary from Sir John Cope to Lieutenant General Guest, whom he had left in command of the few troops around Edinburgh. From Inverness Sir John intimated that he was about to march his army the hundred miles to Aberdeen, there to embark for the Firth of Forth and again seek battle with the Highlanders. Guest must waste no time in sending shipping from Leith to transport him and his men southwards from Aberdeen. But would Sir John's army arrive in time for the relief of Edinburgh?

Two days later officials of the Bank of Scotland at Bank Close off the Lawnmarket had first-hand confirmation of the reality of the Jacobite threat in the person of Lieutenant Ferguson of the Scotch Royals, newly freed on parole by the insurgents in the north and now seeking recompense for Bank of Scotland notes he had unavoidably lost in the King's service. The lieutenant's tale was that with two companies of the Royals he had been ambushed in the Great Glen by the Keppoch MacDonalds, and that he had witnessed the raising of Charles Edward's standard of white and red silk at Glenfinnan, where the country of Clanranald marches with Lochaber of the Camerons. So news of the approaching danger spread throughout the town.

Responsibility for the maintenance of public order, as indicated by the town meeting he had convened in old St Giles, lay with the civic head, the Lord Provost. He was Lord-Lieutenant, High Sheriff, Colonel of that would-be militia, the Train Bands (which existed more on paper than in actuality), Captain of the hundred-strong City Guards with their tricorne hats and muddy-red uniforms, and Admiral of the Firth of Forth. Lord Provost Stewart was of a family of Perthshire gentry, Edinburgh's member of Parliament, a wine merchant with vaults in Leith, a big house at the head of the West Bow looking down on the Grassmarket, and a sarcastic tongue. With his Perthshire family connections, he was, not surprisingly, thought to be Jacobite in his sympathies, perhaps only vaguely so. His abiding concern was, and would be, the well-being of the city rather than that of the Royal House of Stuart. But his enemies on the Town Council and in the town led by ex-Lord Provost Drummond who had fought for King George at Sheriffmuir thirty years past, and was a big man in Edinburgh, made much of Stewart's suspected Jacobitism, and hoped to oust him in the approaching Michaelmas elections. These would be spaced over the month of

*Antoine Walsh, the slaving millionaire, whose ship brought the Prince from France, takes his leave of Charles Edward on the Moidart shore. Portrait presented by the Prince to Walsh after the '45 (Scottish National Portrait Gallery).*

September as the city's merchants and trades in their Guild and respective Crafts chose members of the Town Council to sit alongside the Lord Provost and his fellow magistrates, the baillies. A large body, thirty-eight members in all, the Council's composition had changed little since it had been fixed by the strong hand of King James VI, a century and half past. Essentially, it elected itself.

From its council chambers in the Goldsmith's Hall near to St Giles, and from the taverns to which members adjourned to wet their whistles, the Town Council ran the town. They upheld the preserves of the guild and of the trades, the surgeons and goldsmiths, the wrights and masons to the tailors, cordiners and bonnet-makers. They enforced monopolies big and small, from the privilege of printing newspapers to the monopoly of hiring chaises to the port of Leith. The port of Leith itself they ruled and

*Parliament Close and Goldsmiths' Hall*

the
fisheries of the Forth, the best oyster-beds in Europe. A seat in Parliament at far-off Westminster, professorships at the University and teaching posts at the High School, the filling of Edinburgh's pulpits, all were in their gift. Over this domain the Lord Provost ruled as best he could.

On the day that the Bank officials hearkened to Lieutenant Ferguson's tale of woe, anxious townsfolk petitioned the Lord Provost and his magistrates to raise a corps of volunteers for the defence of the capital. Now the prospect of the Highland horde at Perth resuming its southward march wonderfully concentrated the Law Officers' minds. Overturning their previous ruling they advised that it would indeed be lawful for a corps of volunteers to be raised without King George's prior approval to take arms for the defence of Edinburgh. The following day the Town Council so decided, but it did so with some misgivings. In factious Edinburgh, the Michaelmas elections to the Town Council were approaching; and the petition had been got up by those who wanted to oust Lord Provost Stewart from office by making him appear to be 'soft' on Jacobites.

However, to profess their allegiance to the House at Hanover, on 7 September Lord Provost Stewart and his Council resolved to send King George a loyal address 'at a time when the enemies to your person and government were daring enough to take up arms with a wicked intention to deprive us of our religion, liberty and laws'. This was transmitted via the Duke of Argyll in London, the real source of power in Scotland. In the week that followed, while the Prince's army remained at Perth as a previous Jacobite army had done in the 'Fifteen, the great national rebellion of thirty years past, King George's warrant for the belated raising of an Edinburgh regiment of foot arrived, and a start was made to recruitment. A committee of the Town Council 'to meet at Goldsmith's Hall each day at eleven in the morning and four in the afternoon' was appointed to take subscriptions from the citizenry to pay for the considerable cost involved. The Lord Provost was appointed Colonel of this regiment-to-be. More speedily, volunteer companies were raised from the citizenry, one from the College students; and on Thursday 12 September these assembled in the College Yards. From the Castle's storekeeper were sent down muskets, bayonets and cartridge-boxes, Lord Provost Stewart signing a receipt; and old soldiers were found to teach the volunteers arms drill. But everything depended on the speedy return to central Scotland of Sir John Cope's army, and it had taken time to assemble the shipping at Leith which was to bring it from Aberdeen. As for the town's historic walls, though the College's Professor MacLaurin with his renowned knowledge of mathematics had been enlisted by the Town Council to advise on their strengthening and re-fortification, repair work had been interrupted by the elections that week to the Crafts of masons and wrights. First things first in factious Edinburgh.

*Page from the Loyal Address by the Town Council*

On Saturday the 14th, a horseman brought the long-feared news from Perth. The Highland army had resumed its southward progress; unchallenged by Gardiner's dragoons had forded the River Forth outwith the range of the guns of Stirling Castle, was marching on Edinburgh; was already at Linlithgow. In haste the volunteer companies were told to assemble their four hundred the following morning; and their sergeants and corporals ordered to make into cartridges the casks of powder and ball brought down from the Castle.

On Sunday the 15th Patrick Crichton and the Glencorse parishioners had congregated at kirk as they did every Sunday to savour the Reverend John Wilson's sermons. But that day in Edinburgh there would be none of the usual Sabbath hush.

That Sunday morning both of Edinburgh's banks had been hives of activity; the Bank of Scotland down Old Bank Close and its rival the Royal Bank of Scotland at the foot of Newbank Close on the other side of the High Street. Both were busy sending their reserves of gold and silver coin to the safety of Edinburgh Castle; and the Bank of Scotland had during its previous week been prudently withdrawing its notes from circulation, mindful perhaps of the need to live down the reputation for harbouring Jacobite sympathies which it had earned for itself in previous years. Its rival the Royal Bank, 'the new bank' as it was known, had been established by Royal charter less than a score of years before. Lord Milton, the Lord Justice Clerk, his home at Milton House on the way to Musselburgh, another great mansion in the Canongate, was the Bank's Deputy Governor. Also a Director since the Bank's inception had been John Philp - he who was to summon his wife that morning from worship at Glencorse Kirk. And here, on account of the significant role he was to play in the events of the next six weeks, we must briefly introduce the Royal Bank's Cashier : —one might say General Manager—a Highland gentleman, John Campbell.

He was a grandson of another John Campbell, Iain Glas, the great 1st Earl of Breadalbane. His father had been the third son of Iain Glas, and had died, unmarried, long since. His patron was the now elderly 2nd earl, at his castle in Strathtay and at Holyroodhouse, where the earl in common with several of the Scottish nobility had apartments; he was also an important, aristocratic customer of the Royal Bank. This no doubt helped young Campbell, already showing an aptitude for business, secure the post of second Cashier at the Royal Bank. With the continuing ill-health of the chief Cashier, John Campbell was soon in a position of influence at Newbank Close, and in the July of 1745 he had formally succeeded to the chief post.

Lord Milton the Bank's Deputy Governor, with the Duke of Argyll and Lord President Duncan Forbes, was one of the triumvirate who ruled Scotland for King George. By his influence The Royal Bank rather than its rival was paymaster to King George's army in Scotland and the channel by which such government funding as found its way to North Britain was disbursed. John Campbell's patron, the 2nd Earl of Breadalbane, was not thought to be active in politics, and Lord Glenorchy his eldest son was profoundly Hanoverian in outlook. There should have been no doubt that the Royal Bank would be staunch for King George. But the 1st Earl had been deep in Jacobite conspiracy, both in the affair of 1708 which nearly set Scotland alight in the aftermath of the widely detested Union with England and in the great Jacobite Rising of 1715. In this, at its culmination in the Battle of Sheriffmuir, Breadalbane Campbells had charged victoriously in King James' cause alongside the Clan Donald regiments, Campbells and MacDonalds shoulder to shoulder. In 1745 many of the clan's gentry among the Perthshire hills, like most gentlemen benorth the Forth, and many from Lanarkshire to the Lothians too, would wish Charles Edward well.

Indeed disaffection with London rule, merging into active Jacobitism, was rife in Edinburgh both in legal and mercantile circles, according to the manuscript history of the 'Forty-five which first came to light fifty years ago. This was written in 1747, apparently by a knowledgeable Scottish gentleman with strong Whig sympathies and devout Presbyterian belief, but with many friends and acquaintances among the Jacobites. In Edinburgh, this unidentified author wrote, 'writers, agents, attorneys, clerks and procurators not to say advocates and lawyers' were mostly infected with Jacobitism and wanted the House of Stuart restored in Scotland: these saw a bigger role for themselves if the Union were broken. He might well have added that many like John Campbell of the Royal Bank were from gentry families with Jacobite pasts. The Edinburgh magistrates (but surely not Lord Provost Stewart), like town councillors generally, he said, were 'of a low descent, mean education, little knowledge and small substance', easily swayed by the Jacobites. To the exclusion of all else the merchants were concerned with their own selfish interests, especially the avoidance of government duties by cooperating with smugglers. Few, said this gentleman Whig, saw the paramount 'necessity' to maintain the Church of Scotland in the cause of 'true religion' and its prop, King George's government.

'Saturday, 14 September 1745. On news of the Highland army's approach, all the effects of the Bank were packt up, and partly transported to the Castle this night, per memorandum apart. Sunday, 15th. The rest of the Bank effects transported to the Castle.' That is all John Campbell entered in his Journal for these days. But what were his thoughts?

The Edinburgh of 1745 was still in the main the town as rebuilt within its defensive walls after the burning it had endured from Henry VIII's army two hundred years past. Along the ridge which ran downhill from the Castle was the *grande place* of the High Street dominated by the tall 'lands' housing all ranks and conditions (and rats in the wainscoting) as if on the under-decks of a 90-gun ship. Like roof beams as seen from the ridge-pole, the wynds and closes, abysses among the high tenements, ran down to the waters of the Nor' Loch and the noisome Fleshmarket; on the south side to a busy street, the Cowgate in its ravine. From the upper lands there were enchanting views all around of the green Lothians, the waters of the Forth and on clear days, when the reek from the town's chimneys cleared, the blue Highland hills in the far distance.

Within the *grande place*, the heart of the town lay round the building which had once been the great mediaeval church of St Giles and was now quaintly divided into four Kirks. Next to the laurel-wreathed statue of King Charles II on his charger was the striking baroque building which in its brief effective life had housed the Scottish Parliament. The memory of what had been lived on in the name Parliament Close. Beyond that was the grim tolbooth, the town's prison. Up the slope, towards the Castle, the High Street led to the Lawnmarket from which the narrow winding West Bow, gave the only access to the Cowgate and the West Port, - one of the six gates through the city walls - and so to the highway to the west. Downhill from St Giles, the High Street ran, with a look of magnificence as splendid as any town scene in Europe, travellers from the south would concede, past the ancient burgh cross, past the Tron Kirk with its wooden Dutch steeple which the Town Council had built in the 1630s, past old houses with wooden galleries, curiously carved, towards the lofty turreted Netherbow Gate. Beyond this was the Canongate with its houses for gentry, town houses for nobility and the Palace of Holyroodhouse which for the past sixty years had been bereft of royalty.

Within its narrow compass the Edinburgh of 1745 had a population thought to be approaching the 60,000 mark, and to the concern of its citizens was beginning to run out of space for Christian burial. Throughout the day - except on the Sabbath - all was bustle on plainstanes and causeway. When the clock on the ancient tower of St Giles showed that it was noon merchants gathered round the burgh-cross to collect moneys and exchange gossip, then to adjourn to the taverns down the dark wynds for their meridian dram, as did advocates and Writers to the Signet from Parliament House, town councillors and gentry come to town. All had this in common; though they might write tolerable English, they spoke the old Scots tongue. As evening came in, the noise on the street intensified. Highland chairmen jostled with their sedan chairs, carrying gentlemen to their drinking clubs, ladies from their tea-parties; piemen shouted their wares, and hefty wives hawked 'peas and beans het and warmm'. After dark there was the splash on the pavements of the most splendid street in Europe as stinking slops were decanted from the high lands. And yet, this was the city which could now also boast the finest infirmary in Europe!

The western end of the Cowgate led on to the Grassmarket and the West Port, all under the towering Castle cliffs. Halfway along to the Cowgate Port and the street's eastern end, on the slope rising to the south were the unimposing College buildings put up by the Town Council in the time of King James VI in emulation of the older universities of St Andrews, Aberdeen and Glasgow. Here too were the College Yards where, that autumn Sabbath, the volunteer companies paraded to confront the approaching threat from the west.

One who paraded that morning was Alexander Carlyle, eldest son of the parish minister at Prestonpans, which lies some eight miles to the east of Edinburgh. A tall twenty-three year old, his College years at Edinburgh and Glasgow behind him, Carlyle now had the happy prospect of the same gentlemanly life of a parish minister of the established Kirk which his father enjoyed. Young Carlyle was fond in a

*The Mercat Cross, St Giles and the Lucken booths*

decorous way of dancing and the company of young ladies; and not much given to any disturbing speculation on matters of religion.

He had been on a visit to that then fashionable watering-place, the little town of Moffat among the Dumfriesshire hills, when he first learned that an army of Highlanders with their 'pretended prince' was marching on Edinburgh. At once Carlyle posted to the manse at Prestonpans. But his father was not at home, and in the absence of parental restraint he was off at once to join his College friends in volunteering for the defence of Edinburgh. That had been on Friday 13 September. Now on the morning of Sunday the 15th Carlyle was drawn up with the rest of the bold 400 in the College Yards, to be told by his company commander, ex- Lord Provost Drummond, that along with the dragoons they were to march out of town that very day to face the Highland horde, and, as Carlyle would rather proudly recall in his old age, 'expose our lives in defence of the Capital of Scotland, and the security of our country's laws and liberties'. The Established Kirk, he and his friends had persuaded themselves, would be threatened by the restoration of the Stuarts.

> We were march'd immediately to the Land Mercat [Lawnmarket - the present day spelling reflecting the 18th century pronunciation]', Carlyle continued. 'There Hamilton's Dragoons who had been at Leith, march'd past our Corps on their route to join Gardiner's Regiment [now positioned to the west of Edinburgh, as Patrick Crichton had seen that morning from the top of the Pentlands]. We cheer'd them in passing with a Huzza.

In response the dragoons drew their swords and clashed them together. It was all a great thrill to the students who would be soldiers.

Some watching the spectacle from the windows of the Lawnmarket lands were unimpressed by the bravado:

> While we Remain'd there which was the Great part of an Hour, the Mob in the Street, and the Ladies in the Windows, treated us very variously, Many with Lamentation and even with Tears, and some with apparent Scorn and Derision. In one House on the South Side of the Street, there was a Row of Windows full of Ladies, who appear'd to Enjoy our March to Danger, with much Levity and Mirth Some of our warm Volunteers Observ'd them, and threatened to fire in to the Windows if they were not Immediately Let Down.

Then came the order to march down the zigzag of the West Bow towards the West Port at the far end of the Grassmarket and take the road to the west:

> Marching Down the Bow, a Narrow Winding Street the Scene was Different, for all the Spectators were in Tears and uttering Loud Lamentations; Insomuch that, Mr Kinloch a Probationer, the Son of Mr Kinloch one of the high church Ministers who was in the 2d Rank Just behind Hew Ballantine, said to him in a melancholy tone, Mr Hew, Mr Hew, Does not this Remind you of a Passage in Livy when the *Gens fabii* March'd out of Rome to prevent the Gauls from Entering the City, and the Whole Matrons and Virgins of Rome were wringing their Hands and Loudly Lamenting the Certain Danger, to which that Generous Tribe was going to be expos'd. Hold your Tongue says Ballantine, otherwise I shall complain to the Officer, for you'll Discourage the Men. You must Recollect the End of all Mr Hew, *Omnes ad unum periere* [To a man they all

perished]. This Occasion'd a Hearty Laugh among those who heard it. Which being over, Ballantine Half Whisper'd Kinloch, Robin, if you're affraid you had better steal off when you can find an opportunity; I shall not tell that you are Gone till we are too far off to recover you.

They halted in the Grassmarket, and it was seen that the Company's ranks had thinned; young Mr Kinloch was not the only faint-heart. But those who stood firm were regaled with bread and cheese, and brandy and strong ale from the Grassmarket brewers. Their resolution was not to be long-lasting; while they awaited the arrival of the other volunteer companies, the College Company was descended on by a posse of clergy, their morning services abandoned, the town's fire-bell having sounded as a general alarm. They were led by Dr Wishart, the College Principal 'who call'd upon us in a most pathetick Speech to Desist from this Rash Interprise, which he said was exposing the Flower of the Youth of Edinburgh and the Hope of the Next Generation to the Danger of being Cut off or made Prisoners, and Maltreated without any Just or Adequate Object'. A few of the students remonstrated against these 'unseasonable speeches', but as for young Alexander, 'from that Moment, I saw the Impropriety of sending us out'. So did the sagacious Drummond, their commander, in this, for once, being at one with the Lord Provost. He forthwith marched his Company back along the Cowgate to the College Yards. His courage, Carlyle recalled, was not to be doubted, but he could well be answerable 'for exposing so many Young Men of Condition to Certain Danger and uncertain Victory'. And the Town Council elections were approaching.

Dismissed from the College Yards, Carlyle and his friends gathered in Mrs Turnbull's tavern near the Tron for dinner and continuing dispute about what to do. They agreed that if it became clear that the Town was tamely to be given up they should lodge their muskets in the Castle to keep them out of rebel hands, and then make their way to Sir John Cope's army when it landed at Dunbar or wherever it came ashore at the mouth of the Firth. As John Home, one of the Carlyle's companions would recall, many eyes that evening were on the weather-vanes. Persistent westerlies would keep any shipping out of the Forth. Would the luck of the winds be with Sir John's transports on their voyage from Aberdeen?

Meanwhile the Company reassembled to keep the night watch at Leith Wynd, the weakest point in the town's defences. Some were still angry at the College Principal's pusillanimity, deeply suspicious too of the real intentions of Lord Provost Stewart. He had vetoed proposals to bring cannon and sailors from merchant ships at Leith to fortify the city walls and had been heard to say. 'It would be, "Damn your eyes Jack, fire away and be damned" and so they would fire upon and murder the inhabitants as well as defend the town against the rebels'. Chief of these critics was the aforementioned John Home (who would one day be leader of Edinburgh's *literati* and author of a *History of the Rebellion in the Years 1745 and 1746).*

Carlyle's recollections continue:

> When the Night Watch was Set, all the Company were appointed to Guard the Trinity Hospital in Leith Wynd, which was one of the weakest parts of the City. There we had nothing to do all night, but make Responses every half hour, as the Alls Well came Round from the other Guards that were posted at certain Distances, so that a Stranger who was approaching the City, would have

Thought it was Going to be Gallantly Defended. But we knew the Contrary, for Provost Stuart [sic] and all his Friends had been against making any preparation for Defence, and when they Yielded to the Zeal of their Opponents, they hung a Dead Weight upon every Measure. This we were all Sensible of at the time, and had no Doubt that they wish'd the City to fall into the Pretenders Hands, however Cautiously they might hide their Intentions. At one a clock the Ld Provost and his Guard visited all the Posts and found us at Trinity Hospital very alert. When he was gone, did you not see said John Home to me How pale the Traitor Lookd, when he found us so vigilant?

Not so, replied young Carlyle, still unwilling to believe the worst. Surely it was only the light from the lantern the Lord Provost was carrying that gave him such a pallor. But when they were relieved and Carlyle went to his lodging 'tho' the House was down a Close, the noise [from the High Street] was so great, and my Spirits so much agitated, that I got no sleep'.

Neither could Patrick Crichton find sleep. He had come up to his town lodging in the Lawnmarket after viewing King George's dragoons from the top of the Pentlands. With the prospect of an irruption of Highlanders, this was no time to be away from the Grassmarket saddlery and ironmongery. 'The pannick in the good town increased; every one wish'd for day light' says his journal, '.... running out, running in and running about was all was done'. But, insatiably curious, he had also come up to town to see for himself the stand to be made by the dragoons. When morning came he left the city by the West Port and walked the couple of miles to the humpbacked Colt Bridge over the Water of Leith by whose eastern banks the dragoons were now drawn up. 'Colonel Gardiner I spoke with. He was in bad habit of body ... and his regiment was fatigued having had long marches and watchings for three days before. They look'd very unlike men would stand to it'. Hamilton's squadrons he thought looked better but, he added, 'alas, they were Irishmen!'

The abiding problem was the lack of foot soldiers to support the cavalry. The hundred– strong bewhiskered veterans of Edinburgh's Town Guard and the hundred or so of the new Edinburgh Regiment already raised on the belated arrival of the royal warrant were manifestly not enough. And all the while, he confided to his journal, the rebel army was approaching 'with their bagpipes and plaids, rusty rapiers, matchlocks and fyerlocks, tag rag and bob taile'.

Gardiner, a distinguished Scot, his home at Bankton House near Prestonpans, was known to Crichton. 'I was with Colonel Gardiner about 3 afternoon', he wrote, 'when one of the Scouts came in and said that 400 of the Highland advance gaird [guard] was on the north east poynt of Corstorphine hill'. It was time to go. 'I took leave of Gardener and retired cross the fields and saw the dragoons mount'. But this was not to do battle. Brigadier Fowkes, new arrived from London to take over all command, had cast his professional eye on his meagre infantry resources, and he opted for retreat past Edinburgh towards East Lothian and (he hoped) Sir John Cope's army when it disembarked. The military wisdom of this strategy was not appreciated by the agitated citizenry watching from Edinburgh's high lands as the two regiments of dragoons streamed along the Lang Dykes, the slope on the far side of the Nor' Loch. This was followed by the procession up the High Street to the safe haven of Edinburgh Castle of the Dragoons' baggage and their women. If Lord Provost Stewart had indeed been searching for an excuse to give up the city without a fight, he had it now. 'The clamour arose that it would be madness to think of Defending the Town as the Dragoons had fled', Carlyle recalled. 'The Alarm Bell was rung — a meeting of inhabitants with the Magistrates was Conveen'd first in the Goldsmith's Hall, and when the Crowd increas'd Clamour and Discordance in the High Church.' To this gathering under the ancient pillars of St Giles a letter addressed to the Lord Provost from Charles Edward was now handed in, summoning the Town Council to surrender the City 'and alarming them with the Consequence in case any opposition was made'. For appearances sake, as his unfriends would have it, 'Provost Stewart at first made a scrupulous Feint about reading the letter', but then read out its imperious demand. All idea of Defence was abandoned and it was resolved that a deputation from the Town Council should go out to meet Charles Edward and negotiate surrender. Captain ex-Lord Provost Drummond had his company march up to the Castle to hand in their arms; and Carlyle with the rest of the student-volunteers went their several ways 'not a little asham'd and afflict'd at our inglorious Campaign'. And no one seemed to recall that the City Guard's own armoury still held a thousand muskets ready for seizure.

By the evening of that day the Highland Army was encamped at Gray's Mill in Slateford, to the south of Corstorphine, three miles from Edinburgh. It numbered only a very few thousand; Clan Donald from Moidart and the Small Isles, from Knoydart and Glengarry, from Glencoe, and from Glenspean and Glenroy; Lochiel's Camerons; the Appin Stewarts; some MacGregors. It was about to be augmented by Athole Stewarts, these last recruited by their 'rightful' Duke now back in Scotland with Charles Edward after thirty years of exile; his younger brother, the 'Whig' Duke of Atholl, having quitted his home at Dunkeld House on the approach of the Highland horde. It was also about to be strengthened by Robertsons from the wilds of Rannoch, by Glenlyon Campbells and by more MacGregors from the Perthshire hills. Also from Perthshire came the Duke of Perth's following. That evening Charles Edward took up his quarters in the miller's house beside the water of Leith as it snakes its way from the Pentland Hills. And it was there after nightfall that Lord Elcho joined him.

Elcho, Winchester School educated, handsome and twenty-five years old like the Prince himself, heir to the Earl of Wemyss in Fife, had seen much of Charles Edward during his own Grand Tour of a few years past. This had turned into something of a Jacobite pilgrimage when he reached Rome, and it taught him to revere King James, though he was not over impressed by the Prince and his passion for outdoor sports, seemingly to the exclusion of all else. But the Earl, Elcho's father at Wemyss Castle, was Jacobite and in correspondence with King James at Rome. Elcho without much reluctance had been drawn into the Jacobite net.

However, the passionate Jacobitism of such as Cameron of Lochiel, or of the Duke of Perth, was not in his nature. When the Highland Army entered Perth, he had been nearby, with his father at Elcho Castle beside the Firth of Tay. From there he had written to, but not gone to meet, his acquaintance, the Tweeddale laird John Murray of Broughton who had taken on the role of Secretary to the Prince. As a friend, tell me the true state of the Prince's army, Elcho had asked. Also, what officers has he brought from France to take command? Back came the mendacious reply : the Highland Army is six thousand strong and many more are expected. Murray also represented the elderly commander of carabineers and the middle-aged Irish Captain in the Prince's retinue as 'the Spanish General MacDonald and the French General O'Sullivan'. Elcho, to his lasting regret, swallowed these untruths. On the day the Highland Army marched southward out of Perth, with his father's blessing he rode out of Elcho Castle to join the Prince. But first he went to Edinburgh and saw for himself the confusion of divided counsels there. On he rode into Midlothian, to Preston Hall some miles south of Dalkeith to attend his brother's wedding to Lady Katherine Gordon, the Duchess of Gordon's daughter. On Sunday 15 September, the wedding over, Elcho disclosed to his brother that he was off to join the Prince 'Whereupon', as Elcho's Journal records, 'he took a key from his pocket and bade me to go to his place at Newmills [near Haddington] and take all the money I could find in his bureau. I spent the night there and found 1500 guineas which I took...'.

On the evening of the following day, Monday the 16th, Elcho caught up with the Prince at Gray's Mill, by the Water of Leith, and near the village of Slateford where the Highland Army was lying. 'It was dark and the Prince received me with great cordiality.... The Prince confessed to me he was in the greatest financial distress, not having the wherewithal to pay his army'. Drawing out his purse, Elcho counted out his brother's guineas and gave them to Charles Edward. In their meeting that September night there was a harbinger of events to come. Charles Edward, said Elcho, 'told me... to be on my guard against Lord George Murray [brother to both the Jacobite and Whig Dukes of Atholl] whom he knew had joined with the intention of betraying him'. This *idée fixe* in the Prince's mind, more than any other single factor, was to bring the Rising to its calamitous conclusion seven months later on Culloden Moor.

Later that night to the miller's house where the Prince was quartered there came a deputation from the Edinburgh Magistrates led by 'Old' Provost Coutts to negotiate the town's capitulation. The Prince, with that sureness of touch so much in evidence in the early weeks of the Rising, would have none of it. Edinburgh must receive him as his father's Prince Regent. At the same time Charles Edward sent a force of Camerons, of Clan Donald and of Appin Stewarts under cover of darkness, led by Cameron of Lochiel, to break into the City. For years Lochiel had been the foremost of the Highland chiefs who were devoted to the Jacobite Cause; and at the raising of the Prince's standard at Glenfinnan he had been the first to bring out all his fighting men. For this assault on Edinburgh Lochiel was accompanied by Murray of Broughton the Prince's Secretary. He too had been a leading Jacobite for the past five years, and indeed more than any other is be blamed for the Prince's arrival in Scotland so unattended. Now thirty years old, university educated at Edinburgh and Leyden, handsome of face, short of stature, a hard-up Tweeddale laird whose personal fortunes depended on the success of the Rising, he was to hold tenaciously to his position of influence at the centre of the Prince's affairs. It is in the narrative that Murray wrote in later years after all was lost, that the capture of Edinburgh is best described.

Though Edinburgh's walls were by now undefended, her gates were shut. But before daylight on Tuesday the 17th, Lochiel's men rushed the Netherbow Port when its gates were opened to allow the coach, which had brought back to town the city fathers after their fruitless mission to Gray's Mill, to return to its Canongate stables. The coachman's mind was no doubt on horses rather than Highlanders. When daylight came, a thousand serving-lassies tending a thousand porridge pots in the kitchens of the high lands, Edinburgh found herself in rebel hands.

As an operation of war it had been impressive enough. Led by Murray who knew the terrain well, the attacking force had marched with exemplary discipline past Edinburgh's southern outskirts to position itself in total silence outside the Netherbow Port and in St Mary's Wynd where the city's walls were at their most dilapidated. Lochiel, a Highland gentleman, who by his own admission 'knew nothing of war', had proved his ability as a commander. And while the credit for the rushing of the Netherbow Port belonged to the Camerons, the contingent of Glengarry MacDonells persuaded themselves that it was all their doing; as in regard to himself did John William O'Sullivan, who had also been there and was now exalted from captain to the rank of colonel.

But it is clear from Murray's account that in reality success had been in the balance till the last minute. Daylight was breaking. An attempt to hoodwink the keepers of the gates into believing that a Cameron dressed in a great coat was a servant of dragoons seeking entry, had failed. The Prince's orders that there must be no bloodshed had been explicit; and with daylight coming Lochiel and Murray had been pondering withdrawal to the Salisbury Craigs to await further orders when the Netherbow gate had been so fortunately opened and, as one of Clanranald's officers would recall, 'our people with drawn swords marched quickly up street, no one leaving their rank or order'. They forced their way into the city-guard house near the Tron Kirk, placed guards on all the city's gates, and drew up their main body in the Parliament Close. There Lochiel's regiment had to stand for five hours while keys to the Outer House of the Parliament building were found, and straw for bedding brought in. Meanwhile, well-wishers plied them with food and drink, but obedient to the Prince's and Lochiel's orders, as Murray put it, 'the sodgers would touch no spirits'.

On word reaching Woodhouselie that same morning of the taking of Edinburgh by 'the scurlewheelers', as he derisively termed them using this old Scots term of abuse, Patrick Crichton had hurried to town. Prudently he walked to town, rather than put his horse at risk to predatory Highlanders. As these marched along by the Braid Hills, he came up with 'the cavillcade and all the Highland wifes along with the baggage, and 3 or 4 hundred men as a guard, all in great spirits with the prospect of warm quarters and plenty, upon the kind Lord Provost's invitation'. Like Carlyle's friend, John Home, Crichton had persuaded himself that Lord Provost Stewart had sold the pass.

Then Crichton came up with the farmer at Colinton Mains who had a doleful tale to tell; his horses and carts had been seized and, forbye, the Highlanders had robbed his house of a half-dozen silver spoons. As Crichton came down Canaan Muir [Morningside] he saw, receding in the distance, Charles Edward and his retinue. The farmer there said that the Prince was on foot and in Highland dress with a velvet bonnet; the Duke of Perth had been on his right hand, Lord Elcho on his left 'and all the hill skippers in rank and file'. The Castle had fired three cannon shots which had made them halt, then they resumed their march out of sight of the Castle gunners along Grange Loan and under the policy walls of Grange House. They had come round Arthur's Seat by the south and crossed the King's Park to Holyroodhouse; there again they had been briefly exposed to the Castle's guns but these had not fired. Avid for every detail, Crichton picked up the gossip. At Blackford House the Prince had paused to take wine. On the last stage of his march Charles Edward had learned that Sir John Cope had now landed at Dunbar. With princely sang-froid he had merely said 'Is he, by God?'

*Grange House past which the Highland Army made its entrance to Edinburgh*

The rest of the Prince's small army, the Perthshire gentlemen on horseback not yet to be deemed a cavalry squadron, the baggage, the trail of Highland women, were already on the move from Slateford early that morning when word came that Edinburgh had fallen, with it the joyous news that no less than a thousand stand of arms had been found in the Town Guard's armoury. Nine years later, across the intervening desert of disillusion and broken hope Lord Elcho would recall that morning:

> When the Army Came near town it was mett by vast Multitudes of people, who by their repeated Shouts & huzzas express'd a great deal of joy to See the Prince. When they Came into the Suburbs the Croud was prodigious and all wishing the Prince prosperity; in Short, nobody doubted but that he would be joined by 10,000 men at Edinburgh if he Could Arm them. The army took the road to Dediston [Duddingston], Lord Strathallan marching first at the head of the horse, The Prince next on horseback with the Duke of Perth on his right and Lord Elcho on his left, then Lord George Murray on foot at the head of the Column of Infantry. From Dediston the Army enter'd the Kings park at a breach made in the wall. The Prince Continued on horseback always followed by the Croud, who were happy if they could touch his boots or his horse furniture. In the Steepest part of the park Going down to the Abey he was obliged to Alight and walk, but the Mob out of Curiosity, and some out of fondness to touch him or kiss his hand, were like to throw him down, so, as soon as he was down the hill, he mounted his horse and rode through St Anes yards into Holyroodhouse Amidst the Cries of 60,000 people, who fill'd the Air with their Acclamations of joy. He dismounted in the inner court and went up Stairs Into the Gallery, and from thence into the Duke of Hamilton's Apartment.

The crowd in the King's Park, now thronging the forecourt at Holyrood had seen a slender young man, not quite six foot in height, reddish hair, brown-eyed, princely features, clad in tartan, a blue sash over his shoulder, breeches of red velvet, a green velvet bonnet with gold lace round it and bearing a white cockade. And it felt as if the whole of Edinburgh had been gripped by the high emotion of the moment, the return of a Stuart Prince to Holyrood. But within the Palace, the Great Apartment, built three-quarters of a century past for King Charles II (who never came) wore the sad aspect of neglect; hence the recourse to that of the Duke of Hamilton, the Palace's hereditary Keeper. On entering the Palace, awaiting him were only the unimpressive Earl of Kellie from Fife and a number of Lowland gentry; two veterans of the Fifteen, Arthur Elphinstone and James Hepburn of Keith; from Tweeddale the sixteen-year-old nephew of Murray of Broughton; from Stirlingshire Lord Elcho's prospective brother-in-law, the heir to Graham of Airth; and 'Willie' Hamilton of Bangour, much given to versifying in high-flown Augustan metres. To give something of a much-needed flourish to the occasion Hepburn of Keith stepped forward, drew his sword and preceded the Prince into the Palace. (So goes the well known story given a kind of later-day immortality by that fine Scottish actor, the late Finlay Currie, in the otherwise excruciating Alexander Korda film *Bonnie Prince Charlie*, — though Hepburn's son always denied that his father could have been capable of any such dramatic gesture. But it may well have been so. This was a morning for the casting off of inhibition).

# II

# *Gladsmuir*

While Lord Elcho was meeting the Prince at Gray's Mill the previous evening and the Town Council was momentarily regretting having sent a deputation there to talk surrender — news having come at long last that Cope's transports were off Dunbar — Alexander Carlyle and his young brother had pushed their way through the press of people at the Netherbow Port and left Edinburgh.

In the moonless night the coast road was deserted, the waving whin bushes giving it an eerie feel. They were dog-tired when they called in at Lucky Vint's tavern at Prestonpans and found it crowded with Colonel Gardiner's dragoon officers, as they paused in their retreat to the east, all anxious for news about the whereabouts of the Highland Army. Their fear of Highlanders was all too evident as they assembled their troopers and trotted off along the coast road to Dunbar.

In the morning, Carlyle was joined by two volunteer friends from Edinburgh which they confirmed had now fallen to the Highlanders. Their intention was to waste no time in joining the Royal Army, the word at Prestonpans being that the transports were already landing Cope's regiments at Dunbar. But this brave resolve was deferred by an invitation to dinner at a friend's house with the prospect of whisky punch, claret and burgundy 'which some of us had never tasted' and which their young host feared 'if we did not accept of he would be obliged to give to the highlanders'. So it was late in the afternoon when the three young men set out to walk the dozen miles or more to Dunbar, pausing at 'Maggie Johnston's Publick House' near Haddington for beer and porter. There they had a boozy row with a recruiting sergeant on 'whether the musket and bayonet or the broadsword and target were the best weapons'. Then on in the dark to Linton Bridge where in their bravado they spurned the offer of beds for the night. They pressed on to Dunbar but found it now thronged with Cope's soldiery and offering nowhere to lay their heads. So back to Linton Bridge to knock up the parish minister at two in the morning 'who, taking us for marauders, kept us an hour at the door'. So ended their day of light-hearted approach to war.

Fifteen hours earlier Miss Magdalen Pringle, daughter of a Berwickshire laird, eighteen years old and on a visit to Edinburgh, had watched Lochiel's regiment take formal possession of Edinburgh for the Prince. 'Dear Tib' she wrote to her younger sister back at Greenknowe Tower in the Merse:

## Notes on the Colour Illustrations

*Miniature of Prince Charles Edward Stuart*
This Portrait was given by the Prince to Lochiel at Edinburgh in 1745, and has remained a treasured possession of his descendants. (Courtesy of Sir Donald Cameron of Lochiel. Photograph by Alex Gillespie.)

*Portrait of John Campbell*
This portrait by William Mosman of the Royal Bank of Scotland's Cashier was painted in 1749. (Courtesy of the Royal Bank Of Scotland)

*The Skene Collection*
James Skene of Rubislaw was not Edinburgh born but came to the city from Aberdeen in 1785. A talented amateur artist, he became acquainted with Walter Scott when they were both young advocates in Parliament House, and they soon became close friends. Scott admired Skene's talent as an artist, and suggested that the two of them should collaborate on a monthly publication to be called *Reekiana* which would portray the changing face of the city. Skene would do the drawings while Scott would supply the text. Scott's financial disaster in 1826 put paid to the project collaboration. Skene's manuscript, however, along with 220 superb watercolour drawings, are lodged in the Edinburgh Room of the Edinburgh Central Library. A few of those with particular relevance to the text are included here.

*1 Netherbow Port*
*2 Antient (Ancient) Cross of Edinburgh: Phantom Heralds proclaiming the fate of Flodden Field*
*3 Old Assembly Rooms of Edinburgh's West Bow*
*4 Leith Wynd*
*5 The Trone (Tron) Kirk before the South Bridge was opened*
*6 Antient (Ancient) Porch of Holyroodhouse*
*7 Holyroodhouse*
*8 SW Portion of the Church of St Giles called the Auld Kirk*
*9 Castle Gate*
*10 Parliament House*
*11 Colt Bridge (from which the Dragoons retreated so precipitately on 16th September, 1745)*

Nether Bow Port

10.

Antient Cross of Edinburgh. *Phantom Heralds proclaiming the fate of Flodden Field.*

Old Assembly Rooms of Edin? West Bow.

*Leith Wynd.*

Trone Kirk before the South bridge was opened.

Antient Porch of Holyroodhouse.
pulled down about 1750

Holyrood house

S.W. portion of the church of St Giles.
called the Auld Kirk.
altered 1826.

Castle gate.

Parliament House                          destroyed by a new fr...

A little before twelve o'clock seven hundred or thereabouts of the Highlanders that had taken possession of the town surrounded the Cross and at one o'clock five Heralds and a Trumpet with some gentlemen, amongst them Jamie Hepburn [who had conducted the Prince into Holyroodhouse with drawn sword] ascended the cross and read two manifestos in the name of James the Eight King of Great Britain etc. And at the end of, everyone they threw up their hats and huzza'd in which acclamation of joy they were join'd by all the crowd which was so great I incline almost to call it the whole Town. The windows were full of Ladys who threw up their handkerchiefs and clap'd their hands and show'd great loyalty to the Bonny Prince.

In this (the first recorded reference anywhere to 'Bonny' Prince Charles Edward) Magdalen Pringle added, as if by way of a postscript for the eyes of her staunchly Whig father back in Berwickshire. 'Don't imagine I was one of these Ladies. I assure you I was not'. But then, a little wistfully she wrote 'All the ladies are to Kiss the Prince's hand. I've an inclination to do so, but I can't be introduced'.

King James duly proclaimed, the Highlanders sauntering in the High Street were 'quiet as lambs, civil to everybody and takes nothing but what they pay for'. The only danger they offered was from carelessness with firearms:

Mady Nairne was looking over Lady Keith's window along with Katie Hepburn. On the other side of the street there was a Highland man and a boy standing with a gun in his hand which gun went off and shot in at the window and went in at Mady Nairne's head. Mr Rattray [surgeon] took out the ball and sow'd up her wound. The Prince has sent several messages to inquire after her which has help'd not a little to support her spirits under the pain of her sore wound.

The familiarity with which Miss Pringle here referred to 'Mady' Nairne and 'Katie' Hepburn, both from staunchly Jacobite families, suggests what many other sources attest - the absence at this stage in the conflict of any rancour between gentry families with deep-felt allegiance to the Stuart King, and those like the Pringles of Stichill who stood for King George.

As disgusted with the spectacle as the flowers of Edinburgh had been ecstatic was Patrick Crichton. Entering by the Bristo Port, 'which I saw to my indignation in the keeping of these caterpillars', he observed the sentries' rusty swords and antique guns and that they were busy 'catching the vermin from their lurking places about their plaids'. It was otherwise when he watched the proclamation of King James from a friend's window on the north side of the High Street. 'Comic fars or tragic comedy' it might be, but against his will he was impressed by the spectacle:

All the mountain officers with their troupes in rank and file in order marched from Parliament Close down to surround the Cross, and with their bagpipes and lousy crew they made a large circle from the end of the Luickenbooths to half-way below the Cross... none but the officers' and special favourites and one lady in dress [the young wife of Murray of Broughton] were admitted within the ranges.

Despite the old men and boys interspersed in their ranks with their pitchforks and scythes stuck on to poles, Crichton shrewdly observed that here was 'the most daring and best militia in Europe'. So the Cameron pipers blew, 'a fashion of streamer over their shoulders', the gold and crimson of the emblazoned tabards of herald and pursuivants showing the Royal Arms, quartered after the Scottish form, contrasting with the ancient grey mercat cross round which they stood, and all the while the bells of the High Kirk rang out. Then a profound silence and the reading by Ross Herald of King James' declaration and Charles Edward's manifesto as Prince Regent. 'Thus,' noted Crichton, 'the winds blew from Rome and Paris to work our thraldome'.

Ross Herald was Roderick Chalmers of Portlethen, son to a Kincardineshire laird and Writer to the Signet who had paid with his life for his adherence to the Stuart cause at the Battle of Sheriffmuir thirty years past. He was now accompanied by Islay Herald and Snowdon Herald and by Dingwall and Kintyre Pursuivants. In so appearing they were all defying Lord Lyon, Alexander Brodie of Brodie, a staunch Whig who had fled Edinburgh. The proclamations declaimed by Ross Herald had been, firstly, from King James 'given under our sign manual and at our court at Rome' appointing 'our dearest son, Charles, Prince of Wales to be sole Regent of our Kingdoms of England, Scotland and Ireland with our Dominions'. The second, dated from Paris, was by Charles Edward proclaiming that 'we are now come to execute His Majesty's will and pleasure..... asserting his undoubted right to the throne of his Kingdoms', and promising free pardon for past subservience to the Elector of Hanover (i.e. King George) to all who now rallied to the Stuart cause, the maintenance of the Protestant religion in England, Scotland and Ireland, and much else about the security of the liberties of the people. And all this while the guns of Edinburgh Castle remained silent.

As to the scene in the Palace of Holyroodhouse that day, one turns to the pages of *Waverley* and its delineation by the unparalleled historical imagination of Sir Walter Scott:

> A long, low, and ill-proportioned gallery, hung with pictures, affirmed to be the portraits of kings, who, if they ever flourished at all, lived several hundred years before the invention of painting in oil colours, served as a sort of guard chamber or vestibule to the apartments which the adventurous Charles Edward now occupied in the palace of his ancestors. Officers, both in the Highland and Lowland garb, passed and repassed in haste, or loitered in the hall as if waiting for orders. Secretaries were engaged in making out passes, musters, and returns. All seemed busy, and earnestly intent upon something of importance.

From there the young Edward Waverley, erstwhile captain in Gardiner's Dragoons, was conducted to a presence room, fitted up with some attempt to royal state:

> A young man, wearing his own fair hair, distinguished by the dignity of his mien and the noble expression of his well-formed and regular features, advanced out of a circle of military gentlemen and Highland chiefs by whom he was surrounded. In his easy and graceful manners Waverley afterwards thought he could have discovered his high birth and rank, although the star on his breast and the embroidered garter at his knee had not appeared as its indications.

'Let me present to your Royal Highness.....' said Fergus, bowing profoundly.
'The descendant of one of the most ancient and loyal families in England,' said
the young Chevalier, interrupting him. 'I beg your pardon for interrupting you,
my dear Mac-Ivor; but no master of ceremonies is necessary to present a
Waverley to a Stuart'.

This catches exactly his assured, princely charisma attested to by all who saw
Charles Edward that day. But it was a novelist's invention, not a historians' research
which had a captain in King George's army so spectacularly defect from his allegiance as Edward Waverley had done. Neither now nor later would there be any such.
That, however does not detract from the accuracy of Sir Walter's evocation of the
heightened emotions of the day and of the impression made on all around him of 'a
prince to live and die under'.

Reporting the events of the 17 September, Edinburgh's thrice weekly newspaper,
the *Caledonian Mercury* announced to its readers that:

> Affairs in this city and neighbourhood have taken the most surprising turn
> since yesterday, without the least bloodshed or opposition; so that we now
> have in our streets Highlanders and Bagpipes in place of Dragoons and
> drums.....

So did Thomas Ruddiman the elderly, erudite scholar and Latinist, Keeper of the
Advocates' Library, owner and editor of the *Mercury*, begin to show in print those
strong Jacobite feelings which, with the eyes of the Edinburgh magistrates upon him,
he had up to now been forced to suppress.

Ruddiman continued with a report of the taking of Edinburgh; how the dragoon
regiments had declined battle with the Highland Army at Coltbridge; how this had
provoked 'a general consternation' in the city, and the ringing of the Fire Bell to the
orders of the magistrates summoning a town meeting; how a letter from the Prince
had been handed in to that meeting which had made the magistrates decide to treat for
capitulation and how 'all was very quiet till about 4°clock this morning when, as the
Netherbow was opening a few of the Highland Army entered thereat and was followed by about 1000 resolute hardy-like men' who took possession of the city. 'All
those highlanders,' it observed 'behaved most civilly, paying cheerfully for what they
got and continue to do so.'

Ruddiman went on to describe 'the entry into the Abbey of Holyroodhouse' and
how 'at one afternoon the Highland Party spread carpet on the Cross' and the Herald
proclaimed the King's Declaration and the Prince's Act of Regency. 'All the public
offices continue their business', the report concluded, 'nor is any person molested or
injured in person or property.' The tone was unmistakably Jacobite; throughout
Charles Edward being referred to as 'the Prince' not 'the Pretender's Son.'

Three days later, on the 20 September, the Highland Army marched to meet Sir
John Cope, now known to be marching with his cavalry, infantry and guns towards
Edinburgh. Sir Walter Scott's imagination gives us a memorable depiction of the clan
regiments and the Prince's makeshift cavalry setting out from their quarters under the
canopy of heaven on the slopes of Arthur's Seat to confront King George's army:

> In the front of the column the standard of the Chevalier was displayed, bear-

*The Spottiswoode Amen Glass: a Jacobite drinking class. Air Twist stem, engraved in diamond-point on bowl (The Drambuie Collection) .*

'Amen' drinking glasses ("God save King James I pray / Send him victorious / Soon to reign over us / Amen") were often of Scottish make and date from the 1740s

ing a red cross upon a white ground, with the motto *Tandem Triumphans*.
Many horsemen of this body added to the liveliness, though by no means to
the regularity, of the scene, by galloping their horses as fast forward as the
press would permit, to join their proper station in the van. The fascinations of
the Circes of the High Street, and the potations of strength with which they had
been drenched over night, had probably detained these heroes within the walls
of Edinburgh somewhat later than was consistent with their morning duty. The
leading men of each clan were well armed with broadsword, target, and fusee,
to which all added the dirk, and most the steel pistol. But these consisted of
gentlemen, that is, relations of the chief, however distant, and who had an
immediate title to his countenance and protection. Finer and hardier men
could not have been selected out of any army in Christendom.

But, in a lower rank to these, there were found individuals of an inferior
description, the common peasantry of the Highland country, who, although
they did not allow themselves to be so called, and claimed often, with apparent truth, to be of more ancient descent than the masters whom they served,
bore, nevertheless, the livery of extreme penury, being indifferently accoutred,
and worse armed, half naked, stinted in growth, and miserable in aspect.

From this it happened that, in bodies, the van of which were admirably well
armed in their own fashion, the rear resembled actual banditti. Here was a
pole-axe, there a sword without a scabbard; here a gun without a lock, there a
scythe set straight upon a pole; and some had only their dirks, and bludgeons
or stakes pulled out of hedges. The grim, uncombed, and wild appearance of
these men, most of whom gazed with all the admiration of ignorance upon the
most ordinary productions of domestic art, created surprise in the Lowlands,
but it also created terror.

Then the solitary piece of artillery in the Prince's army was fired:

No sooner was its voice heard upon the present occasion than the whole line
was in motion. A wild cry of joy from the advancing battalions rent the air,
and was then lost in the shrill clangour of the bagpipes, as the sound of these,
in their turn, was partially drowned by the heavy tread of so many men put at
once into motion. They vanished from Waverley's eye as they wheeled round
the base of Arthur's Seat, under the remarkable ridge of basaltic rocks which
fronts the little lake of Duddingston.

The previous day, Thursday 19 September, the Royal Army had begun its westward
march from its camp a mile outside Dunbar. By now young Alexander Carlyle was
with them and he had sought out Colonel Gardiner who, as befitted such a devout
Presbyterian, had taken up his quarters at the Dunbar Manse. Gardiner as one of his
father's parishioners was well known to Carlyle:

He receiv'd me with Kindness, and Invited me to Dine with him at 2 a clock,
and to come to him a little before the Hour. I went to him at half past one, and
he took me to Walk in the Garden. He look'd Pale and Dejected which I attributed to his Bad Health and the Fatigue he had lately undergone. I began to ask
him, if he was not now quite satisfy'd with the Junction of the Foot with the

Dragoons and confident that they would Give a good account of the Rebels. He answer'd, Dejectedly, That he hop'd it might be so, But - and then made a long pause. I said that to be sure they had made a very Hasty Retreat: a Fowl Flight said he, Sandy, and they have not recover'd from their Panick; and I'll tell you in Confidence that I have not above 10 Men in my Regt who I am Certain will Follow me, But we must Give them Battle Now, and Gods Will be Done!

However, at dinner in the Manse, Cornet Kerr, a kinsman of Gardiner's, with the enthusiasm of youth 'spake of victory as a thing certain, if God were on our side', and indeed, the following day on its march to the west the long column of horse, scarlet-clad, foot and field-guns made a brave show.

With them were the student volunteers, now reduced to twenty-five in number. They halted for the night in open country near Haddington, Carlyle and his friends making their way to the town's inn. There, on being joined by their company commander of the previous week, ex-Lord Provost Drummond, they begged him to intercede with the General that they might take their place alongside the red-coats in the line of battle. Cope politely demurred, requested instead that they take the inn's post horses and scout ahead of the army during the hours of darkness. So again Carlyle had little sleep, his task now to venture on horseback as far as Musselburgh. Returned to the army as dawn broke, and able to report that the coast road was clear, he rejoined Sir John on his westward progress.

Familiar since boyhood with the lie of the land, Carlyle was surprised that the General chose not to take the higher ground to the south of their line of march but to keep to the coast road, and halt at a stretch of open country not half a mile from the Prestonpans manse. But this in fact was Cope's second choice as a possible field of battle. Word brought to him that the Highland Army was on the march and already across the Esk at Musselburgh had ruled out his original plan to take up a strong position overlooking that river. So his troops now formed their line of battle south of the village of Prestonpans, on open ground, its corn harvested only the previous day. 'They were hardly form'd,' Carlyle would recall, 'when the rebel army appear'd on the high ground south west of our army about a mile. On the sight of them our army shouted. They drew nearer Tranent and our army shifted a little eastward. All this took place by one o'clock'.

Now followed the high-point of Carlyle's military service. Colonel Gardiner had recommended him to the General for further employment that day. This led to him being asked to 'provide a proper person to venture up to the Highland Army to make his observations' [as to their strength]. So Carlyle prevailed on his father's Church Officer to undertake this mission; he was to return with an alarming account of 'how numerous and fierce the Highlanders were, how keen for the fight, and how they would make but a breakfast of our men'. Then an aide-de-camp came with a request from the General that Carlyle should keep a lookout from the steeple of Prestonpans Kirk. He eagerly complied, and, observing the movement of some hundreds of the rebels to the west, mounted his horse to inform Sir John. It was all heady excitement for young Carlyle. As evening came the Highland Army seemed to settle down for the night. Released from his vantage point, Carlyle called again on Colonel Gardiner 'and found him grave and serene but resign'd', and again all too clearly full of fore-boding. Gardiner ended their meeting 'by praying God to bless me, and [saying] that he could not wish for a better night to ly on the field, and then call'd for his cloak and other conveniences for lying down, as he said they would be awak'd early enough in the morning, as he thought by the countenance of the enemy'; the Highland Army now being separated from them by only the intervening morass.

Carlyle now made his way to his father's manse, finding it crowded with a noisy company of clergymen from the Merse and with volunteers from Edinburgh who had not been close to the action as he had been, yet nevertheless were boasting of their deeds that day. But the excitement of the past seven days had been all too much for him. 'No sooner had I cut up the cold surloin which my mother had provided, than I fell fast asleep... I retir'd directly'. And so it happened that Alexander Carlyle was not able to give posterity what would have been an enthralling account of the battle at day-break, seen from the steeple of Prestonpans Kirk, as in the half-darkness the Highlanders found a way across the morass between the two armies and then in the misty morning light butchered what it did not take prisoner or scatter of the Royal Army, with glory as well as death for Gardiner but for few others of its numbers.

But within a quarter of an hour of the first cannon being fired Carlyle was view-ing the scene of horror from a high point in the Manse garden:

> The Whole Prospect was fill'd with Runaways, and Highlanders Pursuing them –Many had their Coats turned as prisoners, but were still trying to Reach the Town, in Hopes of Escaping. The Pursuing Highlanders, when they could not overtake, fir'd at them: and I saw two Fall in the Glebe. By and Bye a Highland Officer, whom I knew to be Lord Elcho pass'd with his Train, and had an air of Savage Ferocity, that Disgusted and alarm'd – He enquir'd fierce-ly of me, Where a publick House was to be found; I answer'd him very meekly, not Doubting but that If I had Displeas'd him with my Tone, his Reply would have been with a Pistol Bullet. The Crowd of Wounded and Dying now approached with all their Followers, But their Groans and Agonies were noth-ing compar'd with the Howlings and Cries and Lamentations of the Women, which Suppress'd Manhood and Created Despondency.

Carlyle, to his credit, went at once to offer his services at the big house in Prestonpans of [Revenue] Collector Cheape where he found over a score of wounded officers of the Royal Army. To their credit the Duke of Perth and Cameron of Lochiel were showing a proper concern for them; and indeed Elcho's anxiety to find a tavern was probably not to assuage his own thirst but to find ale to sustain the wounded as was normal in the aftermath of an eighteenth-century battlefield. In company with a 'fine, brisk, little, well-dress'd highlander' from the Duke of Perth's regiment Carlyle went off to find the medicine-chests from the abandoned baggage-train of the Dragoon regiments. Down the street came a couple of grooms leading four fine black horses, to be confronted by the Highlander:

> He Drew a Pistol from his Belt, and Darted at the foremost in a Moment, What are you Sir, and whare are you Going, and whom are you Seeking. It was answer'd with an uncover'd head and a Dastardly Tone, I am Sir John Cope's

Coachman, and I am seeking my Master. You'll not find him here Sir, But you and your man and your Horses are my Prisoners. Go Directly to the Collectors House, and put up your Horses in the Stable, and wait till I return from a piece of Publick Service. Do this Directly as you Regard your Lives. They instantly Obey'd.

But the full horror of that morning was brought home to Carlyle when he and his father rode through the field of battle where 'the dead bodies still lay mostly stript - there were 200 we thought'. In fact, of the Royal Army some 350 had fallen; most, literally, hacked to pieces by Highland broadswords. To Edinburgh and the Lothians which had forgotten the realities of the war - the last battle in the vicinity the slaughter at Pinkie, two hundred years in the past - it would be deeply shocking. 'Gladsmuir' was the name erroneously given to the field of battle by the Highland Army. The reverberations of Gladsmuir would be felt nine months later on Culloden Moor.

*East view of Edinburgh Castle in 1745*

The first indication in Edinburgh of the disaster that had befallen the Royal Army that morning was the spectacle of four dragoons galloping up the High Street towards the refuge of the Castle. The devotedly Jacobite Laird of Gask, at whose Perthshire home the Prince had breakfasted only eleven days past, happened to come out of Writer's Court at that moment, and challenged them to dismount. Two meekly complied, but on seeing that he was on his own, fired their pistols at him. Laurence Oliphant of Gask was lucky not to pay for his audacity with his life. At the shocked household at Woodhouselie the word was that others of Cope's scattered cavalry had been seen that morning making for the safety of the Pentland Hills, 'all in froth and foame'.

By the following morning a few officers and about a hundred escapees from the carnage of the battle had also found refuge in the Castle. Their arrival, with wildly exaggerated estimates of the strength of the army which had overwhelmed them, did nothing to stiffen General Guest's resolve. A kindly Yorkshireman who had risen from the ranks early on in Marlborough's wars but had retained his sympathy for the hardships of the common soldier, Joshua Guest had served in Scotland in the defeat of the Jacobite Rising of 1715. In these days army generals did not retire, no matter how old they were. Guest was eighty-five, an invalid and scarcely able to stir from his room though nominally left in charge of what government forces remained in the Lowlands. With the approach of the Highland Army he had been in a flutter, begging advice from the Lord Justice Clerk about what to do - but Lord Milton was now with Cope at Berwick. So was Lord Mark Kerr, the Castle's (sinecure) Governor. The Deputy-Governor was General George Preston, another veteran of King William's and Marlborough's wars, and like Guest an octogenarian. Preston, however, had been the Castle's Deputy-Governor since 1715 and as the rank-conscious would put it, was 'of family, 'with all the self-assurance that implied in the Scotland of his day. Valleyfield is near Culross where the Perthshire border then marched with that of western Fife; and the Prestons of Valleyfield traced their descent deep into mediaeval times. The Deputy-Governor's influence would be crucial, if the tale the great nineteenth-century antiquary picked up from an old lady of Preston's family is to be believed – and Chambers gave it credence. Guest in overall command, as shocked as the new arrivals at Cope's defeat, was for giving up the Castle, maintaining that its garrison was unfit to withstand the rigours of a siege by an army as strong in numbers as the Highlanders were (wrongly) reputed to be. Preston, with a sharper appreciation of what King George's interests required, would have none of this. There must be no surrender.

The 22nd of September was another Edinburgh Sabbath. Again the city's Kirks were silent: the four into which mediaeval St Giles was clumsily divided; the Tron Kirk down the High Street; Greyfriars beside the town's increasingly congested burial ground. Only at the West Kirk (as St Cuthbert's was then known) outwith the city walls but under the guns of the Castle, was there defiance. There, quite unhindered by the victorious Jacobites, the elderly Reverend Neil McVicar prayed for King George. In East Lothian Alexander Carlyle's father likewise exhorted his congregation to be steadfast. He, young Alexander would recall, 'not only pray'd fervently for the King, but warn'd the people against being seduced by appearances that the Lord was with the rebels'. But the Reverend Mr Carlyle did not deliver this exhortation in his Kirk at Prestonpans. More prudent than valiant, or perhaps simply fearful for the safety of young Alexander an account of his services to the Royal Army before the battle, he had taken himself off for that day with his son to the safety of a parish closer to the Lammermuir Hills, leaving Mrs Carlyle to see to the security of the Prestonpans Manse as best she could. And on the evening of this day the Prince

*The Prince, flanked by the Duke of Perth and Lord Elcho, returns in victory to Edinburgh on 22nd September 1745 (Early-Victorian engraving)*

returned to Edinburgh, his army's pipers blazing away at 'The King shall enjoy his own again'.

The great entrance gateway built in the reign of King James V is no more; it was taken down in 1750. But standing in the Outer Court you see today essentially the Holyroodhouse of 1745. The sole reminder of the royal residence King James V had built some two hundred years past was the tower at the northern end of the frontage, cleverly married to the principal quadrangle which had been built in the 1670s with something of the look of a French chateau. Though Charles II never came, averse to Scots as he was from the dosages of Calvinism he had once had to swallow from Scottish divines, his brother who would succeed him, James, Duke of Albany did come in 1678 to remain for four years as a successful viceroy of Scotland. There, in the Great Apartment built for his brother he had held Court. The memory of its brief vice-regal splendour would long remain.

But now in its neglected state it was unfit to receive Charles Edward, James's grandson. However, there was a suite of rooms looking onto the Outer Court which at the time of the building of the Great Apartment had been constructed for Charles II's queen. These had been kept in good order and refurbishment. The reason for this was that on James's departure, 'the Queen's apartment' had been bestowed on the 3rd Duke of Hamilton, as the Palace's Hereditary Keeper. This was no small mark of favour. As Keeper, the Duke had the right to lodging somewhere in the Palace, such as in the apartments on the floor above built for the great officers of state of an independent Scotland, but not to this special suite of rooms at Holyrood. By 1745 successive Hamiltons had come to look on it as their permanent Edinburgh residence (as indeed did the aged 2nd Earl of Breadalbane in regard to his apartments on the floor above). It was to the elegance of this Hamilton suite that Charles Edward had ascended up the Palace's great staircase, James Hepburn of Keith, in his inspired moment, preceding him with drawn sword. It was to these rooms that the Prince now returned in victory.

The ante-chamber which Edward Waverley had seen fitted up 'with some attempt to royal state' lacked the splendour of Canopy, Cloth and Chair of Estate appropriate to a Presence Chamber. But the other rooms were handsome indeed. The panelled walls of the room which was the Prince's Great Dining Room were hung with pictures: a Dutch seascape and a landscape; portraits of the later Stuarts from Mary Queen of Scots onwards; a full-length Kneller of James, Charles Edward's grandfather. There was a new William Adam chimney-piece the Hamiltons had had built only eight years past, and mahogany tables and chairs from the workshop of Francis Brodie, Deacon of the Wrights of Edinburgh (and father of the infamous Deacon Brodie – but that is another Edinburgh story!).

Next to the Dining-Room and within the James V tower was the Prince's Drawing Room. It was here that the Prince's Council met; here he received the Jacobite ladies of Edinburgh. Within the Drawing-Room Charles Edward would see (if the record of a few years later may be relied on) a suite of mahogany chairs, two French 'elbow' (arm) chairs and a large three-cushioned 'sopha'. Curtains of crimson silk and worsted damask framed the views from the big windows of the houses, gardens and tennis-courts of the Burgh of the Canongate. A Duchess of Northumberland, resident in the Hamilton apartments in 1760, would write of 'our Drawing-Room, the place where the Pretender kept all his plans', and indeed the study opening from the room's south-west corner wall would have been a suitable place for the Prince's paper-work.

The bed-chamber of this Hamilton suite was also the Prince's. Its big curtained bed and some of its chairs survive elsewhere in today's Palace. It was in this room that Scotland's destiny – and ultimately Charles Edward's – had been fixed unalterably when the devious 4th Duke of Hamilton, darling of the Scottish 'patriots' in the years preceding the Union with England, had his night long discussions with a secret envoy of Louis XIV of France in 1705. In this the 4th Duke became clear in his own mind that the interests of the House of Hamilton would be better served by Union with England than by the restoration of a Stuart King, and so had became the secret engineer of the Union with England, the saboteur instead of the champion of the Stuart Cause.

Here for the next five weeks a royal court would be maintained 'with great magnificence', as Elcho recalled. Every morning at nine the Prince's Council, the nobility in his army, the Highland chiefs, Sir Thomas Sheridan his Irish confidant, Murray of Broughton, the Prince's Secretary, assembled in the Prince's apartments. As befitted royalty, the Prince, to music playing, dined in public with his principal officers. Also as befitted a Royal Prince, he had had Lord Elcho form a troop of Life-Guards. Each day, in their uniforms of red and blue facings they escorted Charles Edward to the far side of Arthur's Seat where the Highland Army was encamped around the little village of Duddingston out of sight of Edinburgh Castle's guns. In the evening the Prince returned to Holyrood House, and received the ladies who came to his drawing-room. He then supped in public. Generally there was music again at supper, and a ball afterwards.

These were the legendary Holyroodhouse balls in which the Duke of Perth's mother, Lady Nithsdale and the lovely young wife of John Murray of Broughton took the leading roles - and one recalls the words of David Daiches that 'eighteenth-century Scotland danced as it has never danced since'. But, curiously, if any of the many ladies who had learned their steps in the Assembly Rooms off the West Bow and now adorned this brief renaissance of Holyrood committed to writing in later years what they remembered of reels and minuets in the Long Gallery what they wrote has not survived. For some, whose romantic hearts had been given so completely to the Bonnie Prince, perhaps memories lay too deep for tears. What has survived is a passage in Colonel O'Sullivan's report to King James in Rome when all was over, giving a history of the Rising from its beginnings on Hebridean Eriskay in July until the calamity of Culloden nine months later. Three weeks past, at the House of Lude in Perthshire, another of those who had come from France with the Prince would recall of him that '... he was very cheerful and took his share in several dances, such as minuets, Highland reels (the first reel the Prince called for was 'This is not mine ain hoose') and a Strathspey minuet'. But now, at the first of these Holyroodhouse balls, Colonel O'Sullivan would remember:

The Prince went to see the ladies dance, made them compliments on their dance and good grace and retired. Some gents followed him and told him that they knew he loved dancing, and that the Ball was designed for him to amuse him. 'Its very true', says the Prince. 'I like dancing and am very glad to see the ladies and you divert yourselves, but I have now another air to dance, until that be finished, I'll dance no other'.

Another scrap of recorded recollection comes from an Irish harper who had played for the Court at Holyrood. Long afterwards he was asked what he could recall of the Prince. He replied: only his frequently asking 'Is Sylvan here?' This remembers Charles Edward's Italian accent. It may also, incidentally, be taken to indicate his increasing and dangerous reliance on that bluff, middle-aged Irishman, Colonel John William O'Sullivan.

Adept in the arts of propaganda, the Prince's staff – one sees in this the hand of John Murray of Broughton – were quick to put out their own account of the battle, and this was carried in Edinburgh's *Caledonian Mercury* for 23 September, its editor, throwing all reserve aside and assuring his readers that what followed was 'plain fact, not the fictitious dream of a luxuriant fancy'; and that 'it is confidently presumed that the publishing of the same will be highly acceptable to the public.' When the Prince had put himself at the head of his army as it marched out of the King's Park he had drawn his sword and said 'My friends, I have flung away the scabbard'. As it drew itself up for battle amidst the cornfield stubble near Prestonpans he had said 'Follow me, Gentleman. By the assistance of God I will this day make you a free and happy people'. As soon as the signal to begin the attack was given, the Highlanders had pulled off their bonnets, looked up to heaven and made a short prayer. Then they had come on like a torrent, holding their fire on the red-coat lines 'until the closeness of our shot might set their whiskers on fire'. Though Cope's horse and foot had been routed 'it must be owned that the enemy fought very gallantly' before they were forced to run when they could no longer resist. As soon as the victory was seen to be complete the Prince 'mounted his horse and put a stop to the slaughter, and finding no surgeons amongst the enemy dispatched an officer to Edinburgh with orders to bring all the surgeons to attend, which was accordingly done'.

Before giving the names of officers and numbers of men killed on both sides, the editor of the *Mercury* warmed himself with the reflection 'that 2000 highland foot, unsupported by horse and charged in front and flank with artillery and small arms, routed a regular army of above 4000 [sic] horse and foot in an open plain and obtained a most signal and compleat victory with a very inconsiderable loss'. But, Jacobite though he was, he could not but mention the battlefield's scene of horror, the hundreds of corpses from Cope's army, English and Scottish, among the corn-stubble.

# III

# *The Siege of Edinburgh Castle*

The Jacobites had so far been cheered by a summer of unbroken sunshine. 'They have been from their first Rising highly favoured with glorious weather', said the *Mercury* of 27 September, 'The season, even in this month of September, is more mild and comforting than it has been in June for the last half-century.' This must have contributed in no small measure to Jacobite high spirits. Had the Prince been proclaimed in a High Street shrouded in haar, or drenched by an Edinburgh downpour, euphoria would indeed have been dampened.

But Gladsmuir was a false crest. The immediate advance into England which the Prince so ardently wished was out of the question; the common Highlanders' age-old custom of returning to their glens with their booty after victory won, a telling comment on the poverty in which so many lived, had for a while sorely depleted the strength of the Highland Army. The immediate need was to persuade Sir Alexander MacDonald of Sleat and MacLeod at Dunvegan to raise their followings of some 3000 Skyemen for the Cause. The other imperative was to bring pressure on that devious octogenarian Simon, Lord Lovat to raise his Frasers from Stratherrick and the Aird in eastern Inverness-shire. Surely, it was thought, these three must now declare for the Prince. The day after the Prince's return to Holyrood Alexander MacLeod, younger of Muiravonside, the son of a veteran Jacobite now a West Lothian laird who was the Laird of MacLeod's man of business in Edinburgh, also rode north with letters from the Prince, penned by Murray of Broughton, to bring the Skye chiefs to their duty. 'Sandy' MacLeod (who in Hebridean Raasay was memorably to displease James Boswell twenty-seven years later with his loud behaviour) was instructed by Murray, to give it out on his journey north that these two had already declared for the Cause.

Money was the other pressing need. Along with the baggage of the Royal Army, Cope's military chest of £4000 had been seized. A half-a-crown levy on every pound sterling of Edinburgh rentals would shortly be imposed. But this would not be enough. It was imperative that the Prince be able to pay his rank and file the requisite sixpence a day, much more for the clanned gentry. Were the Highland Army to attempt to live off the country in line with the worst practices of continental armies, they would soon lose such popularity as they enjoyed. So John Hay of Restalrig, Jacobite son of another Edinburgh Writer to the Signet, was dispatched with an armed escort to Glasgow, a town now enjoying a new prosperity from the tobacco trade with Virginia, to exact monies from that town's Bailie Nicol Jarvies.

On Wednesday 25 September, four days after the battle, Patrick Crichton went to town where he found 'most of the zealous inhabitants were fled — Highlanders with guns and swords straggling here and there and everywhere'. Edinburgh was complying with the Prince's demand for a thousand tents 'I saw parte go in cartes for Dudeston escorted by a Highland detachment with bagpipes and colours... I saw at Nether Bow a good many of the King's soldiers [from Cope's defeated army, its Highland Regiment in particular] that have listed with them and have white cocades which is the badge of that gange'. The officer prisoners had been paroled after 'they were in first put in the D. of Queensberry's house in Cannongate'. The rank and file were in close custody in the Canongate Tolbooth and its adjacent church, miserable on the penny a day each prisoner was allowed to buy food, but as the *Mercury* for 27 September would report 'the poor soldiers who were wounded at the late battle daily die of their wounds both in town and country, and such or have been able to crawl to town are cheerfully succoured by the inhabitants'. At Duddingston the Highland Army were trying out their newly acquired train of field artillery. 'I heard them all the road as I came home fyring the cannon'. Shoes, stockings and water canteens were being demanded in great numbers from Edinburgh. 'If all the clans come up as is talked of they will eat up this poor place', Crichton glumly concluded.

Alexander Carlyle had now come up to Edinburgh, there to live in the house of a friend from the staunchly Jacobite Seton family (this another instance of the intermingling of Whig with Jacobite) while he equipped himself for the sojourn at the University of Leyden which his father wished him undertake, whatever happened in Scotland. Less circumspect, young Carlyle's friend John Home elected to continue as a volunteer in King George's service and would have some memorable adventures in the months ahead. To Edinburgh people Holyrood had long been known as 'the Abbey', for the Palace of James V had been joined on to the medieval monastery and with later development had taken over the whole site, making the whole of the Abbey its Chapel Royal. It was to 'the Abbey' that Carlyle now went twice to watch the Prince ride off at noon with his escort through the neighbouring St Ann's Yards and along the Duke's Walk (so named from the days when his royal grandfather had held court at Holyrood) to review the Army at Duddingston:

> I had the Good Fortune to see him both Days, one of which I was close by him, when he walk'd thro' the guard to take his Horse. He was a Good Looking Man of about 5 Feet 10 Inches. His Hair was Dark Red and his Eyes Black; His Features were Regular, his Visage long, much Sunburnt and Feckled; and his Countenance Thoughtfull and Melancholy.

'In the house where I liv'd', Carlyle continued, 'they were all Jacobites, and I heard much of their conversation'. They were 'sanguine and uppish', but the word in town on which Carlyle fastened was that the Court at Holyrood was dull, and the Prince melancholy. 'He seem'd to have no confidence in anybody, not even in the ladies who were much his friends!'. No doubt Carlyle heard only what he wished to hear, for the enthusiasm of the ladies of Edinburgh seems to have been undimmed. 'Who would not be transported with the sight of such a loving Prince', wrote a Mrs Anne Dott to a Mrs Jennett Wilson, 'and seeing him sway his sceptre with such power and at the same time mingled with love even to his usurper's subjects... Nothing could give me more pleasure than to see this valiant Prince plac'd upon the throne of his ancestors'. 'Oh, had you beheld my beloved Hero, you must confess he is a Gift from Heaven', wrote Miss Threipland of the Jacobite family at Fingask, on her return from the Court at Holyrood. But there would be others like the redoubtable Mrs Carlyle at the Prestonpans Manse. A young officer of the Duke of Perth's Regiment had been assigned to her after the battle to ensure that there was no harassment by marauding Highlanders. At morning prayers, Carlyle recalled, the ensign turning awkwardly, his broadsword 'sweep'd off the table a china plate with a roll of butter on it':

> Prayer being ended the good lady did not forget her plate, but taking it up whole, she said smiling and with a curstey, 'Captain Brydone this is a good omen, and I trust our cause will be as safe from your army as my plate has been from the sweep of your sword'.

On 29 September John Hay returned from Glasgow with £5500 for the Prince's military chest. But some was in Royal Bank of Scotland notes, and so two days later John Campbell's diary recorded a call at Newbank Close from the Prince's Secretary to demand payment in coin for these banknotes 'and on failyure therof within 48 hours, that the estates and effects of the directors and managers should be distress'd for the same.'

That is an impossible request, Campbell replied. All of the Bank's moneys are lodged in Edinburgh Castle, and the Governor there is denying access. Campbell went on to explain that four days past he and two of the Bank's Directors wishing to conduct banking business had been refused entry to the Castle 'tho' they continued at the gate for about hour'. Murray was adamant. He would give him in the Prince's name a pass through the Jacobite lines now watching the Castle Hill. He hoped that the Governor would give admittance. But whether he did or not, if the payment was not made, the order would be put into execution, and the Directors' homes, with Campbell's own house at Restalrig, 'distressed'.

Thereupon, at Mrs Clerk's tavern down Fleshmarket Close, Campbell met the two Directors in town, one of whom was John Philp, Patrick Crichton's neighbour at Woodhouselie, and they agreed to meet again at the Bank building 'that this affair be further concerted, and if possible money be got out for answering the demand' (which seems a weak-kneed response when it would seem to have been easy to insist that entry to the Castle was not possible). Meanwhile a letter should be sent to General Guest seeking access, after its terms had been approved by Murray of Broughton 'to prevent any mistakes'— which suggests that no hint was to be given as to the true purpose — and the other Bank Directors should be notified.

When they convened the following morning there was a message from Murray that there would shortly be a further demand on the Bank, and when they dined at Mrs Clerk's later that day Campbell was informed that there was now a further £2307 in banknotes to be converted into specie and that it must be done within forty-eight hours. This further demand the Directors likewise agreed had to be accepted, though Campbell says that he expostulated 'about the impossibility of what was demanded':

> ....but he said that all excuses was in vain, for that a gentleman, who understood the business of banking, was with the Prince, who said that there was no difficulty in the thing, for that all the gold and silver must be in baggs of certain sums, and therefore that it was an easy matter, and required no great time to execute this affair, and so the Prince was positive to grant no longer indulgence.

Over a pot of coffee at Muirhead's tavern John Campbell continued discussion with Philp and his fellow Directors. There is in his journal no hint of dissension by anyone about what was now to be attempted. Their fears would not be simply over the practicability of bringing the moneys out. They were also about their own safety in seeking access to the Bank's reserves lodged in the Castle. For the Castle itself, now under active siege, was firing on the town.

It may have had been a measure of the frustration now gripping the Prince and his Council that, in default of knowing what to do next after victory at Gladsmuir, they should now have chosen to harass Edinburgh Castle. On their return to Edinburgh on the evening of 22 September they had posted guards from Lochiel's Camerons in the Grassmarket, and at the head of the Lawnmarket in the Weigh House, to which in this well-regulated municipality traders in butter and cheese brought their produce in more normal times. But the sentries had not sought to interfere with the passage of supplies for the Castle garrison. Alternatively, what lit the fuse may have been old General Preston's response from the Castle to the Prince's demand that he instruct Captain Beavor of the 24-gun frigate the *Fox* and senior officer to the 20-gun *Happy Jennet* and the *Hazard* sloop-of-war, all now in the Firth of Forth, to refrain from obstructing Jacobite movement on the ferries across the Forth to Kinghorn and at the Queensferry: the General had replied that he would rather grant a pass to Hell to any Jacobite who applied.

The capture of Edinburgh Castle, chief of King George's fortresses in his North Britain, would have been a prize indeed for the Prince. In its 700 years of history the castle on its lofty plug of black basaltic rock had been taken by subterfuge, by starvation, by the scaling of its sheer crags, by bombardment and by the failure of will on the part of its defenders. As to subterfuge, there would be no opportunity in 1745 to emulate the feat of the Black Douglases of 400 years past, a surprise attack jamming the portcullis gate at the Castle's entrance. The Highlanders for their part would recall the scaling attempt on the north-facing crags at the outset of the 'Fifteen with complicity on the part of a Jacobite-minded sergeant of the garrison. That had all but succeeded; but in 1745 the northern crags had been made even more formidable by the erection a few years previously of the high angled walls and domed sentry boxes which today look down so impressively on Princes Street Gardens. They had been built with just such an emergency as this in mind. In fortification, if in nothing else, North Britain was ready to resist Jacobite adventure.

There remained starvation and bombardment. In the Castle's three months siege of 1689 when a Jacobite Duke of Gordon held it for King James, the garrison had indeed been starved into submission. But it was now well provisioned, though the

Highland Army did not know this. As to bombardment, in the great siege of 1573 when the castle was gallantly held by supporters of Mary, Queen of Scots, heavy cannon brought to Leith by Queen Elizabeth's navy and then playing on its powerful eastern defences had reduced them to rubble and enabled a successful storming. But Cope's captured field guns were not siege guns, nor would they be any match for the armament now bristling from the great gun-platforms of the Half-Moon and Argyle Batteries and from the guns commanding the Castle's other aspects. Though in his Journal Patrick Crichton noted the rumour that Cameron of Lochiel intended to attempt a storming of the Castle by 120 picked men, with General Preston making a round of the sentries in his bath-chair every two hours to keep them to their duty, nothing was likely to come of that. There was in fact only one alarm on the night of the 25th which occasioned retaliatory panic fire from the sentries on the Castle ramparts. But as the *Mercury* reported this was not Lochiel's men scrambling up the castle rock, only the herd of goats that lived and fed there!

On the evening of 29 September a letter from the Castle came to the Lord Provost at his house at the head of the narrow winding West Bow: unless communication between the Castle and the Town was kept open the Castle's cannon would fire to dislodge the Highland guards; and the Castle's guns would 'distress' the city if it did not furnish provisions for the garrison. A town meeting of sorts was there and then called to the 'New Church' within the walls of old St Giles; and next morning six deputies from the Town Council waited on the Prince at Holyrood to show him the General's letter. Charles Edward gave them a reply in writing to take up to the Castle saying that 'he was equally surprised and concerned' at the barbarity of the intention of 'bringing distress on the town'. If this threat is carried out, Charles Edward continued, I will see to it that General Preston's house of Valleyfield is likewise distressed. This reply in turn was conveyed by the Town Council's anxious deputies to the Castle, evoking the immediate response from the old warrior there that the guns of the *Fox* would be turned on Lord Elcho's clifftop Wemyss Castle, also on the coast of Fife, should Valleyfield suffer. In this strange civil war of a sort General Preston did however agree to a six-day truce for instructions to be sought from London as to any draconian measures of retaliation on the town.

But the truce broke down. This may have followed on the discovery of an attempt to smuggle information into the Castle from the government side, perhaps from the commander of the frigate in the Firth. A supply of butter for Guest had been allowed by Murray of Broughton (who, no doubt for reasons of policy had previously struck up a friendship with the General), milk products being all that failing octogenarian's stomach could tolerate; and the offending letter was concealed in a cask of the General's butter. On the afternoon of 1 October the Highland sentries at the Weigh House fired *in terrorem* on people carrying provisions to the Castle. Straightaway the Castle's guns responded, with both cannon and small shot, damaging houses on the Castle Hill which the Highlanders had occupied, wounding some of them and also a hapless servant-lass. Next day, 2 October, the Prince had a proclamation put up all over town forbidding on pain of death any communication between town and castle.

It was in the middle of this escalating violence that John Campbell with his group of Bank directors and colleagues sought access to the Castle that they might meet the

Highland Army's demands for coin. But first they equipped themselves with a pass through the guards at the Weigh House, this obtained from a meeting with Cameron of Lochiel, in his new-found role as Governor of Edinburgh whom they met at Mrs Clerk's. On the morning of 3 October the little band, led by Campbell waving a white flag, made their way through the Cameron guards and into the Castle. The Board of Ordnance had recently built a new house in the solid contemporary style for the Castle's Governor, with wings for the Deputy-Governor and Master-Gunner. (It serves today as the Officers' Mess). It was here that the Royal Bank quartet met the Generals:

> On our arrival at General Guest's lodgings (which is the Governor's new house) the directors and I went in, told him our errand in general was to get into the Royal Bank depositories to do some business, and General Preston having come in at that instant, he was likewise told the same. After some short conversation we left the two Generalls, and proceeded to the place where all the Bank things are lodg'd, and executed the affairs we came about.

In telling the generals that their purpose was simply 'to do some business', Campbell and his colleagues, would, to say the least, seem to have been less than frank. More about this shortly.

The excitements of the day were not yet over. For the six hours of their stay in the Castle there was the noise of cannonade against 'Livingston's Yards', a house near the West Church where a Jacobite outpost had been positioned to prevent supplies to the beleaguered garrison up the Castle's steep eastern cliffs. The Bank party saw the return of 'one Watson, a soldier 'who was let down these cliffs by rope when he surprised the Jacobite outpost, single-handedly killed several, set the house on fire and returned with the help of his rope into the Castle, 'where he was received with loud huzzas for his valour'. As they left the Castle, Campbell and his friends watched a sally being got ready which was to complete Private Watson's good work.

Campbell's diary entry for this momentous day continues:

> Before I went to dinner [at Lucky Clerk's] I waited upon John Murray of Broughton, Esq., [this would be at Holyrood] and told him I was come from the directors to acquaint him that they were ready to exchange current coin for their notes, in terms and in consequence of the two several demands made upon the Bank by way of protests and certification, on which he appointed six oclock at night to receive the money at my house [Restalrig].

There, well away from prying eyes, the money was handed over to Andrew Lumsden, Murray's young depute-secretary:

> and so we parted about eleven oclock at night, having drunk one bottle of wine during our business. The net sum paid was 3076ld.

In the next few weeks John Campbell would hand over to Murray of Broughton and his minions a further £3600 in gold coin from the moneys they had brought down on 3 October. Multiply these figures eighty times or so for present day values!

For years after, every detail of the siege of Edinburgh Castle was discussed again and again round Edinburgh dinner tables. John Home, who as a leading-light of Edinburgh's literati was to compile his carefully researched *History of the Rebellion in the Year 1745,* would assert as fact that General Preston's whole purpose throughout was to deter the Highland Army's southward departure from Edinburgh, in view of the pressing danger to King George and his Ministers that this would coincide with a cross-channel invasion by France's huge army. Such an invasion had been close to embarkation at the beginning of the previous year, and it would be all but undertaken by King Louis' renowned Irish Brigade and other troops under Saxe's command in the months ahead. Home also cited an elaborate plan of disinformation put out by General Preston which was intended to give the Prince's Council the false impression that the Castle's supplies were running low and consequently that surrender was imminent, and so ensure a prolongation of the Highland Army's stay in Edinburgh in their vain hope of bringing about by starvation that which want of siege guns had prevented happening by assault in early September. Had General Preston known the destination of the guineas now uplifted from the Castle (which the Prince, for one, wanted for the invasion of England) he would surely have sent John Campbell and his colleagues away empty-handed, if indeed he had not clapped them in the Castle's prison. The conclusion is inescapable: Campbell and his Directors deceived the Generals. So one looks at the handsome, smiling countenance of John Campbell, his figure swathed in tartan, as the portrait of this proud Gael, painted in 1749 only three years after the wearing of tartan was banned, hangs today in pride of place on the walls of the Royal Bank's boardroom in Edinburgh's St Andrew Square. One remembers his Jacobite ancestry and recalls his frequent visits to Holyrood during the occupation to dine there in Jacobite company, remembers too that his patron, that erstwhile Jacobite, the 2nd Earl of Breadalbane, received the Prince in his own apartment on the upper floor of Holyrood, and one wonders where the Cashier's deepest loyalties lay, or whether the Earl in a last surge of Jacobitism influenced his conduct.

It may well have been that, with the eyes of their competitors for the Bank of Scotland upon them, the need for the Royal Bank to cover up its reluctant or otherwise 'bank-rolling' of the Highland Army worked in Campbell's favour and that of his Directors. There would be no recriminations. A long, distinguished and untroubled career as the Bank's Cashier was to follow, even though the Bank's Deputy-Governor, Lord Milton, Lord Justice Clerk, on his return from Berwick to Edinburgh in November, as John Campbell's diary briefly records, 'found fault with almost every part of the directors' conduct' during his own enforced absence. Indeed he would; and it may have been the embarrassment to my Lord Justice Clerk, had the full story come out, let alone the embarrassment had the Earl of Breadalbane been unmasked, which were the determining factors in maintaining silence.

Now matters came to a climax, as the, Edinburgh's monthly periodical, *The Scots Magazine* for October, would record. In 1689 the Duke of Gordon could not bring himself to use the Castle's guns to break the three-months siege, for fear of the havoc they would create in the town. General Preston had no such inhibitions:

> On the 4th at noon, notice was sent to the inhabitants to remove from the North-parts of James's court, and places adjacent, lest some balls might chance to come that way. A few hours after, a terrible cannonading began. When it became dark, a party sallied out from the castle and set fire to a founding-house, and another house, which was deserted by the inhabitants. This

occasioned a great consternation. Mean time the salliers threw up a trench cross the castle hill; and, to prevent any interruption, scoured the street with cartridge-shot from some field-pieces placed on the castle-hill; by which a merchant's book-keeper and another person were killed, and severals wounded. Before their return, the soldiers pillaged some of the houses that had been deserted.

The firing continued next day, and distressed the inhabitants exceedingly. Bullets did execution at the Flesh market close-head, so that no body was safe to stand on the street. Some houses were shattered. Those who lived exposed to the castle, removed; and carried out the aged and infirm at the imminent hazard of their lives. Great numbers that lived in places that were in no hazard, were likewise so frightened, that they ran out of town, not knowing whither. Several of the inhabitants sent off their valuable effects, and a good deal of them were lost in the confusion. It was a very affecting scene.

Patrick Crichton, concerned for his town house in the Lawnmarket, was an eye-witness to all this:

I went in October 4 and stayed all night with Thoma [Thomas?] in owr howse in Lanmarket, above the old Bank Closs. The Castle thundered till 11 or 12 at night. I saw them demolish a hows in Castle hill. Saturday the 5 was the hottest work to escort there provisions. The Highlanders stood lyning the north syde of Lanmarket the soldyers from there trinch shot down the Lanmarket and I with danger gott down from my closs to Libertons waynd [wynd] head and saw a treadsman in a blew frock had been just shot lying his brains dashed owt and in his blood. He had been peeping by a fore stair and was killed forgenst the west end Loockenbooths [Luckenbooths] north syde the High Streat. I went to Cannongate to Mr Blair's, Thoma essayed to return to owr howse and came to Libertone Waynd head, but ball were going so throng he durst not adventur. The Castle gott up there [their] barrels of ale and provisions up the Castle Waynd [Wynd] than retired to ther trinch and so to the garison, and abowt twelve Thoma with hazard gott in to owr howse and secured owr windows. This night I hear the great guns fyred and demolished parte of the Weigh howse. ..... This was a melancholy shean [scene] this streat battell, all shops shut, evry body scared off the streats except here and ther one skulking and runing. The Cowget [Cowgate] full of cartes with plenishing and so at Nether Bow and all down the Cannonget; had this continued the Prince his exorbitent tax cowld not be gott levied.

That night, under cover of a high-sounding proclamation from Holyroodhouse deploring 'the murders which were committed upon the innocent inhabitants of the city by the inhumane commanders and garrison of the castle' which, had he wished, would have entitled him to take reprisals against the perpetrators, and contrasting his own humane concern for peoples' lives with the Castle's 'barbarity', the Prince called off the blockade. For all these fine words, the Rising had suffered its first major reverse.

Meanwhile, all was not well with the Prince's Council, as it met each morning in the Prince's Drawing Room at Holyrood. Lord Elcho watched the wrangling increase:

His Royal Highness the prince of wailess ansure
To the Gentlmen who were Sent Deputies from
the City of Edinbrough with a Letter from General
Guest threatning. that unless the Cummunication
Betwixt the City and Castle was opened. they would
fire upon the City

Gentlemen

I am Equaley Suprised and Concerned at the barbarity
of these orders yt have ben signifyed to you from the Castle
And which those who Command in it Say they have
Recived from the Electore of hanover. at the Same time
that they own they have Six weeks provisions Left
if he Look't upon you as his Subject he wold never
Exact from you what he Knows it is not in your
poure to do. and Should we out of Compassion
to you Comply with this Extravagant Demand
of his. he might as well Summon us to Quite the
Town. and abandon those Advantages which providence
has Granted us by Crowning the valoure of our troops
with Such Signal Success I Shall be heartley
Sorey for any Mischief yt May befall the City. and
Shall make it my peculiar Care to Indemnify you in
the most ample Maner. In the Maine time. I Shall
Make full represals upon the Esteates of those who are
Known to be open Abetors of the gearman
Gouerment. if I am forced to it by the Continuance
of these Inhumanities

Hollyroodhouse Septr 30
Charles: P: R                1745

*The Prince deplores the bombardment of Edinburgh (The Drambuie Collection)*

The Prince in this Councill used Always first to declare what he was for, and then he Ask'd Every bodys opinion in their turn. Their was one third of the Councill who's principals were that Kings and Princes Can never either act or think wrong, so in Consequence they always Confirmed whatever the Prince Said. The other two thirds, who thought that Kings and Princes thought sometimes like other men and were not altogether infallible and that this Prince was no more so than others, beg'd leave to differ from him, when they Could give Sufficient reasons for their difference of Opinion. Which very often was no hard matter to do, for as the Prince and his Old Governor Sir Thomas Sheridan were altogether ignorant of the Ways and Customs in Great Britain, and both much for the Doctrine of Absolute monarchy, they would very often, had they not been prevented, have fall'n into Blunders which might have hurt the Cause. The Prince Could not bear to hear any body differ in Sentiment from him, and took a dislike to Every body that did, for he had a Notion of Commanding this army As any General does a body of Mercenaries, and so lett them know only what he pleased, and they obey without inquiring further about the matter. But as they were Irish They had nothing at Stake, The People of Fashion that had their all at Stake, and Consequently Ought to be Supposed to Give the best advice they were Capable of, thought they had a title to know and be Consulted in what was for the Good of the Cause in which they had so much Concern; and if it had not been for their insisting Strongly upon it, the Prince, when he found that his Sentiments were not always approved of, would have Abolish'd this Council long ere he did.

This was a bitter disappointment: the more so since, as Elcho later recalled in his Journal, as he repeated, and deepened these strictures, up till then Charles Edward had been the hero-Prince who had 'borne himself well at the head of the second line at Prestonpans, and had shown great moderation at the time of his victory'.

Amidst all these events, where did Lord Provost Stewart stand? Writing in the 1820s, Robert Chambers noted the Edinburgh tradition that the Prince had made a nocturnal call on the Lord Provost at his big house at the head of the West Bow, and the popular embellishment of this tale which would have had a sally from the Castle almost entrap the Prince there. Like the matching tradition which would have had the Prince calling on the aged Countess of Eglinton at her house near the Netherbow Gate, Chambers found the tale of this night-time visit between Prince and Provost hard to accept. So, perhaps, should we. What is known as fact is that Lord Provost Stewart was kept in custody by the Highland Army for the first week of the city's occupation.

Stewart, in any event had had other pressing considerations. He and his fellow magistrates were up for re-election by the end of September, but two of the baillies, the Old Provost and the three Old Baillies with the Dean of Guild, Treasurer and all the merchant councillors had either left town like the ministers of Edinburgh's Kirks or refused to attend. So on 1 October the Lord Provost and those who were left accepted that new elections were impossible, and that they must demit office, leaving Edinburgh without magistracy or Council.

# IV

# *'It was a noble attempt'*

### (Samuel Johnson to James Boswell about the march to Derby)

'O lass, such a fine show as I saw on Wednesday last'. This was Magdalen Pringle now under the Prince's spell, writing to her 'Dear Tib' about the view she had of Charles Edward on 9 October.

> I went to the Camp at Duddingston and saw the Prince review his men. He was sitting in his tent when I first came to the field. The ladies made a circle round his tent and after we had gaz'd our fill at him he came out of the tent with a Grace and Majesty that are inexpressible. He saluted all the circle with an air of grandeur and affability capable of charming the most obstinate whig....

Did she mean Papa, back in the Merse?

> .... and mounting his horse which was in the middle of the circle he rode off to view the men. As the circle was very narrow and the horse very gentle we were all extremely near to him when he mounted, and in all my life I never saw so noble nor so graceful an appearance as His Highness made. He was in great spirits and very cheerful, which I have never seen him before. He was dressed in a blue grogrum coat trimmed with gold lace and a lac'd red waistcoat and breeches. On his left shoulder and side were the Star and Garter, and over his right shoulder a very rich broadsword belt. His sword had the finest wrought Basket hilt ever I beheld, all silver. His hat had a white feather in it and a white cockade and was trimmed with open gold lace. His horse was black and finely bred (it had been poor Gardiner's). His Highness rides finely.

Perhaps Miss Pringle had it in mind that, as well as sister Isabella, disapproving family in Berwickshire might read the letter, as she added:

> Indeed in all his appearance [he] seems to be cut out for enchanting his behold-ers and carrying people to consent to their own slavery in spite of themselves. I don't believe Cesar [sic] was more engagingly formed nor more dangerous to the liberties of the country than this chap may be if he sets about it.

Charles Edward's cheerfulness on which Magdalen Pringle so remarked belied his difficulties. Some accessions of strength to his army there had been. In the first days of October Lord Ogilvy, the handsome heir to the Earl of Airlie, had joined with six hundred men; the Jacobite veteran, John Gordon of Glenbucket had come with Grants and Farquharsons from the hills of Aberdeenshire and Banff; and bodies of Camerons and Keppoch McDonells from Lochaber and the wilds of Rannoch, having now 'stashed' their winnings from Cope's baggage train at Gladsmuir, had rejoined. In her visit to Duddingston Magdalen Pringle had also watched the arrival of the revered and elderly Lord Pitsligo from Buchan. He had come 'with a good many gentlemen, well mounted and a great many servants with them'. (Lord Pitsligo she thought an odd figure. 'He's like an auld carrier', she told Tib.) Cluny Macpherson would bring out his clan as soon as the Strathspey harvest was over. But in the north Lovat still would not commit himself, and the arrival in Inverness of Lord Loudoun, with the continuing influence there of Duncan Forbes, would soon put a dampener on the general Jacobite enthusiasm which had burgeoned as the news of Gladsmuir spread. From Skye, only the old chief of the MacKinnons with his small clan was answering the Prince's summons, though MacLeod at Dunvegan came within an inch of doing so, and Sir Alexander MacDonald too was sorely tempted.

Nor was there quite the response from the Scottish aristocracy there had been in the Fifteen. Then, so many had joined the Earl of Mar's standard that rebellion had the appearance of a great national uprising for King James and against Union with England. But the attainders in the Hanoverian retribution that had followed the Rising had struck at many noble families. For others, Jacobite loyalty had weakened with the years. So from Kenmure Castle in Galloway the son of the Lord Kenmure who had been executed after the 'Fifteen now came to Holyrood - and went home. So did the son of the Nithsdale of 1715; he had been egged on by his Jacobite wife, but courage failed him when he reached Edinburgh. The Earl of Buchan would have been a fine catch; he was coaxed by his friends into the Prince's presence, but for him too discretion outdid valour. Nor was the Earl of Traquair anywhere to be seen, though he had been a founder member of 'The Concert of Gentlemen' which had paved the way for the 'Forty-Five in the earlier years of the decade; and although the Earl of Kilmarnock would join, this was partly due to his own acute financial straits. Disappointing too was the continuing silence from Hamilton Palace, though not seven months past its young Duke, in whose Holyrood apartment the Prince was now living, had joined enthusiastically enough with Murray of Broughton and Edinburgh Jacobites in loyal toasts at Walker's Tavern on the birthday of Charles Edward's younger brother. It was also becoming known that since the last week of September the British army, recalled from Flanders to meet the Jacobite threat, had begun to land in the Thames and the Tyne. There was indeed an air of unreality about this civil war in that communication remained open with England, and the *Mercury* reported week-in, week-out, the movements of King George's army as it gathered to confront 'the Young Pretender'.

Sometime during those weeks of the Jacobite occupation of Edinburgh, the young Jacobite, Robert Strange, had made the only authenticated portrait of the Prince as at that date. From Strange's engraving an Edinburgh miniaturist painted the portrait of the Prince in Highland dress, blue bonnet, white cockade, tartan of red and black with a yellow stripe. This miniature the Prince presented to Cameron of Lochiel (and today it is a cherished relic of the 'Forty-Five at Achnacarry).

Meanwhile the *Caledonian Mercury* was doing its best to keep up Jacobite spirits. To remind its readers of a past Whig atrocity, it took to reproducing the report from the 1690s of the Committee of Inquiry of the Scots Parliament into the Massacre of Glencoe. And the Prince's review of his army, which Magdalen Pringle had watched on 9 of October, it reported by carrying the jaunty, not altogether truthful communiqué 'from the Scots Army at Duddingston':

> This afternoon the Prince reviewed that part of his army which is encamped here. His Royal Highness appeared in Lowland Dress. Before the review was over the Rt. Hon. the Lord Pitsligo came into the camp from Linlithgow at the head of a squadron consisting of 132 Knights, Freeholders and landed Gentlemen, besides their servants all extremely well mounted and accoutred: They are all gentlemen of experience and are mostly above 40 years of age. There came in at the same time 6 Companies of Foot, raised in the Shire of Aberdeen by the said Noble Lord Pitsligo.
>
> N.B. The Lord Pitsligo's Squadron are all in Highland Dress, amounting in all to 245 men.

The Earl of Kellie, the communiqué continued, had returned from Fife 'and brought a considerable body of men with him'. The Prince was about to form a Regiment of Light Horse, 'composed of Gentlemen who are all to be habited in Highland uniform'. (It was this adoption of Highland dress by the whole of the Prince's army which was to lead, in the punitive aftermath of the Rising to the prohibition of the wearing of tartan). The *Mercury's* report concluded:

> They continue beating up for recruits all over the neighbourhood; and as trade is at a stand, vast numbers come into enlist. [untrue]
>
> Yesternight the Rt. Hon. My Lord Ogilvie mounted the Guard upon His Royal Highness, at the head of above 100 brave fellows of his regiment, colours flying, and drums beating.

Overall, in reality, the response was disappointing to Jacobite hopes. But then, on 14 October, by means of a Dunkirk privateer which had slipped into Montrose harbour, there seemed to come deliverance in the arrival at Holyrood of one Alexandre Jean Baptiste de Boyer, marquis d'Eguilles, a secret envoy from the King of France. At once Charles Edward's resolve to march his Highland Army into England revived.

The marquis was not a 'career diplomat', had perhaps been picked by d'Argenson, Louis XV's Foreign Minister, precisely for this reason, to maintain his secret cover. Now middle-aged, widely travelled in Europe, and an officer in the King's Service, a good-looking man as a Jacobite lady would see him, he had the qualities needed for this special mission. His instructions were precise and two-faced. Find out the Prince's intentions and the strength of his army, but do not claim to be the King's ambassador. 'The King, in principle, promises help and sends his good wishes, but has no intention of coming out openly for the Prince until his ultimate success is certain'. Though accredited to the Prince by the King of France d'Eguilles was warned that 'it is required that his commission be kept secret and that he passes himself off in Scotland as a French officer who has gone there out of his own sense of adventure'. In his own hand, d'Argenson wrote in the margin of these instructions 'Not to be given the title of the King's Minister'. For Charles Edward and Sir Thomas Sheridan, d'Eguilles was to represent the French King. For everyone else he was to pass himself off as a French officer come to Scotland out of his own appetite for adventure.

His instructions continued to labour their main point (which eerily foresaw the outcome of the 'Forty-Five). However much the King might wish to assist the Jacobites in their threatening a revolution, 'that is not to say he would blindly support whatever plans they or their Prince might adopt [i.e. the invasion of England by the Highland Army] without their having regard to the calamitous and disgraceful consequences that might ensue'. But all this was written before news of Gladsmuir could reach France. D'Eguilles first learned of the Jacobite victory from the master of a merchant vessel as his privateer approached the coast of Scotland. He had now to anticipate his master's reaction to the news of that resounding Jacobite victory.

The privateer that carried d'Eguilles was *L'Espérance* of Dunkirk. She also carried powder, and arms for 1100 men. On two other privateers were embarked six big brass cannon which might serve as siege artillery. Delayed by adverse winds it was not until the morning of 26 September that they all sailed from Dunkirk Roads. With d'Eguilles there sailed on *L'Espérance* Lieutenant Michael Sheridan, nephew to Sir Thomas, the Prince's confidant, to act as interpreter, for the marquis had no English.

It was a difficult ten days voyage to Scotland as they contended with storms, and then, off the Angus coast, had to elude the attentions of the North Sea Squadron of the Royal Navy. But there they also had a chance encounter with a merchant ship which gave them the news of Gladsmuir and, thanks to her complaisant master, pilotage into Montrose Harbour. Here d'Eguilles ordered a speedy disembarkation, took possession of that astonished Angus burgh, and marched inland to Jacobite held Brechin. Within two days word of this success had reached Edinburgh, and 200 Athole Highlanders were mustered under command of the Laird of Gask to deter any sally from Stirling Castle which might impede the southward progress of the passengers of *L'Espérance*. Edinburgh was reached on 14 October and on the following day in his drawing-room at Holyrood in audience with the Prince and Sir Thomas Sheridan, d'Eguilles revealed the true nature of his mission to Charles Edward.

As d'Eguilles reported to d'Argenson in a report dated the following day, the Prince's reaction had been immediate 'I leave in a week', he had said, 'I am marching straight to London. If your army make a landing and create a diversion, England will be ours within a couple of months. But if by mischance this landing does not take place, or is made too late, everything will be in vain'. In response d'Eguilles was careful to make no promises. He suggested that before attempting a march into England the Prince should await whatever was the French response to the despatch he, d'Eguilles, would now send back to his masters in France about the intentions of the Highland Army. It would, he added, be difficult to make a march into England coincide with a French descent on the Channel coast. The Prince responded that even if French ministers did not give the order to invade England until the marquis' despatches had arrived 'there would still be time for it will take a month for me to close with the enemy'. On the evening of the following day there was a second audience with the Prince. Again he emphasised the necessity of speedy help from France, and he asked that it be led by his younger brother, the Duke of York. But his desperation showed in his exasperated outburst to d'Eguilles 'Cannot I count on an early French landing?. Tell me the truth'.

To Louis XV, the Prince had already written 'Monsieur mon oncle, I have just received with great pleasure the assurances of affection and assistance which your Majesty has given me by means of the Marquis d'Eguilles whom I find a most agreeable person. It is my hope that with that assistance I will bring to a happy conclusion this enterprise which God has already so visibly blessed'. He continued: 'I must repeat what I have said to d'Eguilles. There is no time to lose, and I can now neither withdraw or to delay. So I beg Your Majesty to hasten as much as possible the help you are going to give me. If you do so, I am sure that the war will be over and peace return to Europe.' To d'Argenson, Sir Thomas Sheridan wrote in the same vein. 'Now is the time for decisive action (*des grande coups*)', he wrote. And the Prince, blithely ignoring d'Eguilles' instructions that he must appear as a mere soldier of fortune, presented him with studied ceremony to his court as Monseigneur de Boyer, ambassador from the court of the King of France, the harbinger of a French invasion from their Channel ports to Sussex, or to the mouth of the Thames. As he dined in public at Holyrood Charles Edward had *Monseigneur l'ambassadeur* seated with him, along with the Duke of Perth.

D'Eguilles now set about the task of ascertaining the real strength of the Highland Army. He made a calculation from the number of tents he saw at Duddingston, and this led him to overestimate the Army's strength, and report accordingly to Paris. But he was clear-eyed about Jacobite prospects, as he reported to d'Argenson on 23 October, 'Even should they win further battles, they are lost, Monseigneur, should the French not make a landing'

The Prince's letter to Louis XV failed at first to get off by the west of Scotland, and was delayed. D'Eguilles' despatches went off speedily on Dutch vessels to Holland, the chargé d'affaires at the Hague having been warned to expect them and send them on at once to Paris.

Meanwhile, Edinburgh was almost tranquil. The guns of the Castle, 'that damn'd angry bitch' as Magdalen Pringle had heard a Highlander describe it, were silent again. The Jacobite correspondent of a Kincardineshire laird wrote, 'they light up a bonfire every night to prevent anyone approaching the Castle and are extremely alert'. The main danger on the streets wrote Magdalen, mindful of Mady Nairne's misfortune, came from the accidental discharge of the muskets the Highlanders would forever carry with them. In these mid-October days, as James Maxwell of Kirkconnel, a new recruit to Lord Elcho's lifeguards, would recall, tradesmen made a good thing out of equipping the Highland Army for whatever campaign lay ahead. (Was the Grassmarket saddlery of Patrick Crichton one such business?) With the colder nights of autumn the camp at Duddingston had now been broken up and the Highland Army dispersed between the town and the Canongate, the White Horse Inn at the foot of the Canongate accommodating many of its officers. There were also strong detachments at the Inch and Restalrig, Leith and Newhaven to watch the roads to the south and the east, and the naval frigates in the Forth, this coastal watch being reinforced by nightly patrols along the seashore from Cramond to Musselburgh by Elcho's cavalry. So a typical Order of the Day for mid-October had 'Lochyell in

Lieth; Athole, Ardsheal and M'Lachlen in Duddistown; Keppoch and McKinnon at Inch; Duke of Perth at Restalrigg; Clan Ronald at Newhaven; the north country ffoot in Mercer's house at Lieth'. But these dispositions were constantly changed, which served the triple purposes of keeping the troops alert, disturbing their liaisons with the 'Circes of the High Street', and concealing from any government spies the army's overall continuing weakness in numbers.

Meanwhile, too, Patrick Crichton had learned to his dismay that King Louis' France, probably the Bourbon monarchy in Spain as well, were thought to be about to mount the seaborne invasion of England. This news came on top of his daily concern at the thieving up and down Midlothian by a gang of Highlanders, sporting the white cockade. They were plundering at will, demanding money with menaces, terrifying households all along the Linton and Peebles roads. In reality, they were probably MacGregor desperadoes, unwanted auxiliaries to the Prince's cause; and at Holyroodhouse Lord George Murray was acutely concerned at the bad name they were giving the Highland Army. So, significantly, was John Campbell of the Royal Bank, who begged an officer he knew of the Glenlyon detachment to bring them to heel, we may suppose likewise to preserve the Highland Army's good name.

But Crichton was deeply depressed. Even worse than the loss of property to the marauders was the continued silence in Edinburgh's Kirks on the Sabbath, the clergy having astutely resolved on this, reckoning rightly that their flocks would feel badly about the lack of their weekly dosage of revealed religion, though from his first day in Edinburgh the Prince had made it known that they might preach and pray as they wished. In his heaviness of spirit, Crichton addressed his Maker direct; Edinburgh's affliction was surely divine retribution for the city's past misdeeds, especially for those abominations, the performance of stage-plays, the weekly dances in the Assembly Rooms and the musical concerts in a building down St. Mary's Wynd:

> October 12. This is now the fowrth silent Lords day in Edinburgh. Look O Lord upon the manyfold desolations of that place and make them in it consider ther manyfold former abominations. How do the walls mourn for the stage plays dancing assemblies and consorts of musick, their fullness of bread and lawghter is turned to sackcloth and ashes. In the midest of it ther is no magestracy nor rule in the place. It is as the caldron and the inhabitants as the flesh in the pott. Yet O Lord hear the many importuning prayers are put up by Thy remnant for owr deliverence, and make now a full end, for both citie and cowntry abowt are in owtmost destress and terror and it is time for Thee to work Lord, that we be not as Sodom and Gommorow the cities Thou overthrow in Thy wrath. O Lord, make our enemies, for they are risen up against Thee, make them as Zeba and Zalmuna. Make their carcases fall as dung to fat the land for they have brock all the lawse of hospitality and humanity.

Crichton's appeal to the Almighty was rather more blunt than that of the elderly Reverend Neil McVicar at the West Church outwith the city walls who on Sabbaths prayed that a heavenly crown might soon be given 'to this young man, ye ken wha' I mean, wha seeks an earthly crown'. Crichton's prayer continued in the language he imbibed weekly at Glencorse Kirk:

> Art Thou not it who brock Rachab in pieces and in 1688 and in 1715 wounded the dragon. Lett these appearances our fathers have told us of and which

our eyes have seen be now bread to Thy people this September [sic] 1745. Be Thou O Lord on our syde for it is time for Thee to work when our strenth is nothing and our Councilers infatuat, and when we have been as men that dream. Let our captivitie [be] turned back and spoyll Thow those that spoyll us and scatter them in Thine anger O Lord God of hostes. Lett the virgin dawghter of Zion lawgh them to scorn. Water Thy heretage with Thy ordinences and lett there be no more silent Sabaths in Edinburgh.

But even Crichton had to concede that there was comedy of a sort in the meeting of Highlands with Lowlands on the streets of Edinburgh:

George Balentin, minister of Craigie in Airshire, came to us to see his freinds, left his horse at Woodhouslea and walked to town afoot. He went down to Mr Blair's in Cannonget and was detained supper; and passing at Nether Bow Port with his great freise ryding coat the Highland gaird did not stop him but it struck on Lumbsden a sone of Lumsden the writer and grandchild to the Episcopall minister and a volunteer with his white cocad and his sword under his arme.

We have already met Andrew Lumisden, depute-secretary to the Prince, collecting the Royal Bank's gold from John Campbell.

It struck Lumsden in the head that Mr Balantin was a spye and he follows him up and chalanges him, and requris him to go the Guaird. Our freind George walks on with him and askes if he had any warrant to carry him to the guaird. Lumsden said he had not. Upon this Balenten, seeing him a young lad like a beau and that no Highland men were in vew, snaches his sword from under his arme and Lumbsden runs off and calls out, but Georg being near Cant's Close head, where his fathers howse was, goes streight home. In a little come a strong detachment of Highlanders. Mr Balentin took the alarme and the house being up two pair of stairs he tyed the sheets of the bed to ane easie chare and goes out at the window and escapes. In his droping the window he hit upon Mrs Ferguson's window who lives below and brock the glass.

The house on which he had dropped in was that of Murray of Broughton's mother-in-law.

She called owt in surprise to her servants that all the Highlanders were entering her howse by the window, and the Highland gaird hearing this alarme in her howse came in to the Secretary's lady's mother's howse and saw the sheets hung and cut off as far as they cowld reach. Mr James Balentin's servant keepet his door closse, but they gott a smith and forced it and when they came in they said they belived he was fled they sought for but they wanted the sword. They searched but found it not and did not more harme.

The Minister of Craigie took refuge in a friend's house, lay low for a couple of days, then returned 'under cloud of night' to Woodhouselie; and young Lumisden's affronted pride was assuaged by the return to him, through an intermediary, of his fine silver-hilted sword.

Sir James Steuart of Goodtrees — Goodtrees then pronounced 'Gutters; and today covered by the tide of Edinburgh municipal housing — was Lord Elcho's brother-in-law, and esteemed the cleverest man of his generation, the driving intellect for

Scottish Jacobites. He had joined the Prince in Edinburgh, and in mid-October he compiled a second proclamation for Charles Edward, a vast improvement on the stilt-ed wording of the earlier one which had been read out by Ross Herald on the day Edinburgh fell to the Highland Army. This second manifesto addressed directly the discontent so widely felt, Church of Scotland clergy excepted, at London rule, the corruption by which Government ministers maintained their position, the accumula-tion of national debt from Britain's participation in European war, seemingly in the sole interests of King George's Hanover. It also promised a repeal of the Act of Union of 1707 which was bringing Scotland, it argued, no advantages, many handicaps.

But the repeal of union with England and the revival of a separate Kingdom of Scotland, would open the way to a restoration of the House of Stuart to the Scottish throne alone, with England going her own Hanoverian way. Such was the outcome which at heart most of the Prince's Council desired. Charles Edward would have none of it. For him it was, as Lord Elcho for one was beginning to recognise, 'the three Kingdoms or nothing'. The simmering dispute over this first came to a head at the meeting of the Prince's Council on 22 October. News had arrived from the south that Field-Marshal Wade was now on the point of marching northwards from Doncaster to confront the Highland Army. Charles Edward proposed that his army should forthwith march into England 'where, he said, he was sure all the Country would join him'. Elcho's narrative takes up the story of this last final act in the drama of Edinburgh under Jacobite occupation. It is not difficult to picture the scene in the Prince's drawing room, the imposing James V Gatehouse and the houses of the Canongate glimpsed through the big windows, but all eyes on the Prince as he argued in his accent with its foreign tinge that he had only to appear in England for the peo-ple to look on him as their deliverer and join him in chasing the usurper George back to Hanover; and that Gladsmuir had confirmed that regular troops of the British army would not fight against him as 'he was their natural Prince'.

Nor is it difficult to picture the anxious faces confronting the Prince. Donald Cameron of Lochiel, Alexander MacDonnel of Keppoch and the other Highland chiefs in near-despair at the prospect of a march into the unknown; into an England Lochiel, for one, had never even visited. Young Clanranald and the still younger Angus MacDonell of Glengarry would be too tongue-tied to voice their fears; others would be ill-at-ease at being in open dispute with their Prince. But Lord George Murray, in rising anger, was their spokesman. 'Our army is only five and a half thou-sand strong,' he said. 'It is not possible to force the English to accept your Royal Highness as their Prince and we do not as yet know whether they will support you. It will be time enough to march into England when your friends send for you. As Wade is marching his troops northwards let him do so and let us fight him in Scotland. This will leave the coast clear for the cross Channel invasion which M. de Boyer says is daily to be expected.'

That day's Council ended inconclusively with Charles Edward saying again, old Sir Thomas Sheridan at his right hand growling in agreement — 'that he was sure a great body of English would join him upon his entering their country, that everybody in London was for him and would receive him as he had been joyfully welcomed in

Edinburgh'; and with Lord George replying icily that 'everybody wish'd it might be so; and wish'd that he might soon have authority for saying so.'

When the Prince met his Council at nine the next morning he began by stating 'that he would go to England and was resolv'd upon it'. But opposition continued to be general, excepting only Sheridan and the young Duke of Perth, who never spoke against the Prince on any count. However Lord Elcho, though his dislike of the Prince was growing daily, felt that the families of Catholic Lancashire, which he knew, would rally to his standard. But he was uneasy at what d'Eguilles had told him privately; Elcho with his excellent French would have found it easy to get his confidence. Louis would help restore the Stuarts to Scotland, the French 'ambassador' had said, 'but that it was all one to him whether James or George was King of England'.

Charles Edward now cleverly changed tack. 'Let us leave Edinburgh', he said, 'and march southwards to the Borders. This will be better for army discipline and lessen desertion'. With relief and unanimity the Council welcomed this apparent concession to their views. 'To have continued longer at Edinburgh would have been very improper', wrote Murray of Broughton. 'The Highland army, little accustomed to the effeminacy so common in town might be debauched by women and drink which would render them less able for the fatigue they must of necessity go through'. There was also the Edinburgh climate to consider. 'The rains which in that season of the year falls very much in these parts might naturally occasion diseases they are little acquainted with in their country'. But the Prince had not wavered from his purpose. He now 'caused it put about that he was going to join his English friends and the French landing'.

That night the Prince summoned the leaders of his army to his room and proposed that they extend the march to the Borders by crossing into Northumberland to do battle with Wade there. When Lord George Murray opposed this for the reasons he had already given, Charles Edward said, 'I find, gentlemen, that you are for staying in Scotland and defending your country, and I am resolved to go to England'. There had to be deference to the Prince's views, so Lord George proposed a strategic compromise. 'Let your army march into England if you must,' he said, 'but into the hilly terrain of Cumberland rather than the east coast plain. There in Cumberland is ground fitter for Highlanders to do battle. Let Wade come to us there. His troops will be fatigued by its long march north and by its trudge through the Pennines, all in November weather'.

To this the Prince was slow to give assent though there was here a clever concept which might well have given the Prince somewhere in the Pennines the victory he so ardently wished, and with it the capture of Newcastle. But when the army left Edinburgh there was still no agreement about its objective; and still dismay among many, Cameron of Lochiel especially, that to leave Edinburgh and Scotland would expose their friends there to Whig malice and governmental retribution. Lochiel's recently discovered narrative of the '45 is eloquent on this.

While this debate was continuing, in the last week of October there had cast anchor off Leith the 50-gun *Gloucester* flying the flag of Rear-Admiral Byng, and with him Captain George Rodney's 40-gun *Ludlow Castle*. With the *Fox* and the *Happy Jennet* frigates, the *Hazard* sloop war and a number of transports, they made up the North Sea Squadron which the Admiralty had assembled to cut off the help from France for the Highland Army which had been arriving through Montrose. 30 October was King George's birthday, and Byng marked the occasion with a 120-gun salute, clearly heard at Woodhouselie. With his other pressing concerns the Prince may have taken little notice, but he should have done so. The North Sea Squadron would be fatal to his fortunes: Culloden, six months away, would be fought out of his desperation that more French help could not get through.

To avoid Byng's ships Sir James Stewart of Goodtrees now went north to embark for France from Stonehaven, his mission to represent the Prince at the Court of Louis XV, now that there seemed real hope of a cross-Channel invasion. As the night of 31 October came on, the Prince quitted Holyrood at the head of Elcho's Lifeguards and Lord Pitsligo's Horse. He lay that night at Pinkie House where, seven weeks past, he had slept after Gladsmuir. Next day the army assembled at Dalkeith and adjacent Newbattle. There arrived thirteen brass cannon landed at Montrose from France and ferried across the upper Firth at Alloa, also Cluny Macpherson's 300, 'as handsome men as any in the army'. Conscious that the army was short of surgeons, the Prince had John Rattray - he who had attended to Mady Nairne's wound - roused from his bed and pressed into service. The Highland Army began its southward march, the Prince, on foot, a Highland targe on his back, at the head of the column that marched over Soutra Hill. Somewhere in the column was the Marquis d'Eguilles, conveyed in the Prince's solitary coach. In his last report to d'Argenson he had said that the march into England was now the only course open to the Prince's army which had now run out of money. 'All the money in Edinburgh is in its castle, and that sent by the Spanish has been captured. All that the Prince has raised himself is used up [and, indeed, at sixpence a day for the rank and file, much more for the officers, that would not have been long in happening]. I have had to put up with the insolent and suspicious ways of the people among whom I live,' he continued, 'their divisions among themselves, their short-comings and above all their indolence, the main weakness of their army. But happily, I can console myself by relying on their courage, their pride and the terror they inspire in their enemies'.

Patrick Crichton watched another column as it marched by Roslin Moor and Auchendinny Bridge across the Esk. 'I saw them with my prospect distinctly on their long march along the muir, horse and foot.... They have a troop of gentlemen in huzare dress with furred caps, long swords or shabbers [sabres], and limber boots. The Secretary Murray's lady equipped herself in this dress with pistols at her syde sadle, and her cap distinguished with a white plumish feather. They halted Saturday at Greenlaw and had entertainment from Mrs Philp.' Perhaps her guards from the Appin Regiment against marauders had passed the word that there were good quarters to be had at Greenlaw from the wife of the Royal Bank Director.

For all the misgivings of its leaders, the Army's hopes were high. On 10 November, Katie Hepburn wrote from Edinburgh to a friend. 'Papa writes us they had crossed Tweed, was all in great health and spirits'. The 'noble attempt' had begun. Throughout, Charles Edward had kept his arrogant dignity, demanding loyalty, disdaining, as with the Earl of Buchan, to wheedle support from the faint-hearted.

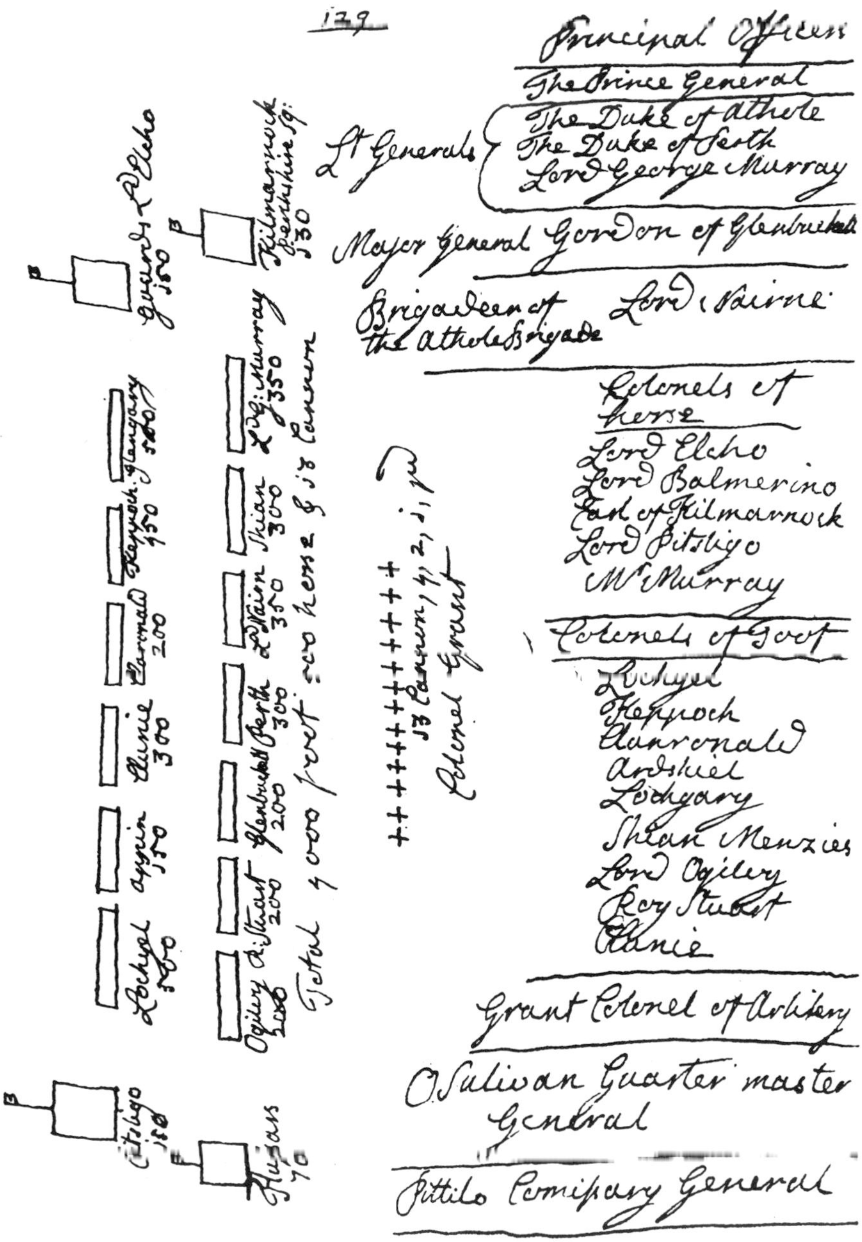

129

Principal Officers

The Prince General

Lt Generals { The Duke of Athole
The Duke of Perth
Lord George Murray

Major General Gordon of Glenbucket

Brigadeen of the Athole Brigade — Lord Nairne

Colonels of Horse
Lord Elcho
Lord Balmerino
Earl of Kilmarnock
Lord Pitsligo
McMurray

Colonels of Foot
Lochyel
Keppoch
Clanronald
Ardshiel
Lochgary
Shian Menzies
Lord Ogilvy
Roy Stuart
Clunie

Grant Colonel of Artillery

O Sulivan Quarter master General

Pittilo Comissary General

*Diagram labels:*

Guards d'Elcho 160

Kilmarnock Perthshire Sqr 350

Lord Murray 350

Shian 300

Glenbucket Perth 200 300

Ogilvy Ardshiel 200 200

Lochyel Appin Clunie Clanronall Glengary Glengary 350 350 300 200 350 300

Total 4000 Foot 200 horse & 13 cannon

13 cannon, 19, 2, 21, 9m

Colonel Grant

Strivigo 160

Hussars 70

*"Papa writes us they had crossed Tweed, was all in great health and spirits." Lord Elcho's sketch of the army which marched to Derby (Courtesy of the Earl of Wemyss)*

# V

# *Aftermath*

The immediate aftermath was ugly, and brutal:'This is a melancholy town, not a Highlandman to be seen,' wrote a Jacobite lady from Leith on the 11th November. 'The Prince went from the Abby on Thursday the 31st October and Friday the first of November the whole of the Highland Army was gone from this place and on Saturday the Castle soldiers was sent down on the Town, and on the collour of searching for Arms they have done great damage and plunder. They have destroy'd the appartment the Prince was in, tore down the silk bed he lay in, broke and carried off all the fine gilded Glasses, Cabinets and everything else'.

There being no civil Government in town, there were other excesses. The Duke of Perth's lodging in the Canongate was ransacked, and other houses of known Jacobites likewise suffered. The soldiery also set about the wife of Cameron of Lochiel 'used her in the rudest manner calling her Bitch and Whore, and had the impudence to spit in her face'. In retribution for the carnage among the corn-stubble at Prestonpans 'They also went to the infirmary and beat up the poor Highlanders, twist about their Arms and legs that was set after being broke at the late Battle, tore open their wounds so that their shrieks were heard never so far'.

On November 13 Lord Milton, the Lord Justice Clerk, the other judges and the coterie of government officials who had fled to Berwick, all returned to Edinburgh. The following day General Handasyde with two regiments of foot and the dragoon regiments which had bolted at Gladsmuir marched through the Netherbow Port. On 6 January General Hawley, appointed to command in Scotland, reached Edinburgh with ten battalions of foot and more dragoons. By then the Highland Army had marched to Derby, and had retreated skilfully to Scotland to join the French rein-forcements which had evaded the naval blockade of the east coast ports and raised Jacobite hopes that the whole of the Irish Brigade might get through. But the Prince had come north by the western road through Clydesdale to Glasgow, not to Edinburgh, and was now encamped near Stirling.

After his humiliating defeat in the driving rain and gathering darkness of a January afternoon on Falkirk Muir, Hawley was superseded by the Duke of Cumberland, King George's second son, a portly young man and a good soldier. He had fought bravely, and been seriously wounded at Dettingen; and as the King's younger son he had commanded, and almost won, at Fontenoy. The young Duke hastened north, took up quarters prepared for him at Holyrood — the bed Charles Edward had quitted — and left early in the morning of the next day for the relief of Stirling Castle as the Highland Army began its retreat to the north. He departed the Palace in style, driven to the West Port in a coach drawn by six horses lent him from his elegant new Adam house near Queensferry by the Earl of Hopetoun. There at the West Port, mounting his grey charger, to great applause the Duke rode off to Linlithgow to join his army. Whigs were delighted with his brief visit. 'The arrival of H.R.H. has done the business' Lord Milton wrote to the Duke of Newcastle, King George's Prime Minister in London.

But Cumberland seems to have formed his own view of Edinburgh. No doubt he had heard of the rapturous welcome given his Stuart cousin in September, and of the Holyroodhouse balls. He would probably regard the unopposed taking of the town by the Highland Army as want of loyalty on the part of the City Fathers. Perhaps he had learned how one of Edinburgh's two banks had financed the Jacobites. That few of Edinburgh's citizens had joined Colonel John Roy Stuart's so-called Edinburgh Regiment for the southward march did not appease his anger. Culloden fought and won, from his Army Headquarters at Inverness he ordered a signal act of humiliation to 'disloyal' Edinburgh. Fourteen of the Highland Army's standards, including the Prince's own one of white and red silk, all these a reminder of how complete had been the rout of Culloden, were brought to Edinburgh and burned at the Cross where 'King James the Eighth' had been proclaimed ten months before. 'The Heralds and

*'The Heart of Midlothian'*

Trumpeters etc, escorted the common executioner who carried the Pretender's colours, and thirteen chimney sweeps who carried the rest of the colours to the Cross. There they were burnt one by one, the herald always proclaiming the names of the commanders to whom the respective colours belonged'. This can have given Edinburgh no pleasure. Nor did it please his royal father: George II gave his son a smart reprimand, for he had wanted the captured standards paraded through the streets of London. Cumberland's venom against Edinburgh found one further outlet. To his father he proposed that she should cease to be Scotland's capital, that honour being accorded to reliable, Whiggish Glasgow!

Edinburgh's premier status was indeed now under threat. At Westminster, Lord Chancellor Hardwicke, with his great influence in government, was arguing forcibly that English law and English judiciary must now be applied throughout Scotland, and he was only thwarted in this by some clever politicking on the part of that arrant Whig, but good Scotsman, the 3rd Duke of Argyll. However, on Cumberland's return south on his journey towards the adulation of London and the strains awaiting him there of 'See the Conquering Hero Comes', he spent a day in Edinburgh. There he was met at the West Port by the cheering, fickle, Edinburgh mob and in the absence of any Town Council received a delegation of the Merchant Guild, and from them a commemoration gold box.

King George's army had performed badly at Gladsmuir and at Falkirk. With the flurry of court martials including that of Sir John Cope which followed the end of the Rising there could be no exception for Lord Provost Archibald Stewart, Lord Lieutenant, Captain of the Town Guard and Colonel of the Edinburgh Regiment that never was. On going up to Westminster in all innocence as Edinburgh's member of parliament, he had been clapped into the Tower of London before being brought back from there to Edinburgh over a year later to stand trial for dereliction of duty. There was some malice in this, the Whig party in the Town Council being now dominant and George Drummond, Lord Provost once more; and in the eyes of London ministers this was now the second time in recent years - the Porteous Riots being less than ten years past - that Edinburgh's Provost and magistrates had been weak-kneed when the King's authority was challenged. Stewart was tried late in 1747. In reality all he had done was to attempt to keep Edinburgh an open city in time of civil war; the culprit for the fall of Edinburgh was the Union settlement itself which, while robbing Scotland of her historic Privy Council, had failed to replace it with the means of countering armed rebellion. So the Edinburgh jury, the Duke of Argyll as Lord Justice-General presiding, unanimously acquitted Stewart,. Curiously, nothing was said about his failure to get the town's armoury into the Castle's safe-keeping, Archibald Argyll perhaps felt that least said was soonest mended. To Hanoverian eyes, however, there was a hero in the saga of the occupation, the aged, ailing Guest. After Culloden he was carried to London in a horse-litter to receive the nation's thanks, and within the year, burial in Westminster Abbey. General Preston received no recognition whatsoever. In that year of Hanoverian jubilation all Scots, including even Duncan Forbes and the Duke of Argyll were under a cloud.

John Rattray, by the intercession of Forbes, his golfing crony, was pardoned; he had been captured at Culloden. But members of the Honourable Company of

Edinburgh Golfers in welcoming him back would also mourn Lt. Col. Robert Biggar, 'Gigantic Biggar' as the Honourable Company's bard had described him in praise of his prowess on Leith Links; he had been killed at Falkirk at the head of the 37th Regiment of Foot. On the other side of the divide, though the Elphinstone family had long given up their estate of Barnton to the west of the city, Edinburgh honoured the memory of the Jacobite peer, Lord Balmerino, who met death so steadfastly on Tower Hill in 1747.

The Jacobite prisoners in Edinburgh Castle had by then been taken to Carlisle for trial and disposal by the gallows or transportation. In Edinburgh itself, as throughout Scotland, there was intense anger as word of the Royal Army's barbarities at and after Culloden came through. In that year of 1746 in London the young Tobias Smollett, perhaps alerted by his mother in Edinburgh as to what was being perpetrated in Lochaber, wrote the words of what was to be in 'North Britain' a popular song entitled 'The Tears of Scotland':

> Mourn, hapless Caledonia, mourn
> Thy banish'd peace, thy laurels torn!
> Thy sons, for valour long renown'd,
> Lie slaughter'd on their native ground;
> Thy hospitable roofs no more
> Invite the stranger to the door;
> In smoky ruins sunk they lie,
> The monuments of cruelty........
>
> What boots it then, in every clime,
> Through the wide spreading waste of time,
> Thy martial glory, crown'd with praise,
> Still shone with undiminsh'd blaze?
> Thy tow'ring spirit is now broke,
> Thy neck is bended to the yoke.
> What foreign arms could never quell,
> By civil rage and rancour fell.

But in Edinburgh there was no reign of terror in the years that followed, provided Jacobite sympathies were not flaunted (and just how widespread these had been may be illustrated by a receipt, discovered years afterwards in the charter-chest at Prestonfield House on the outskirts of Edinburgh, home to a family of no known Jacobite sympathies, from 'Holyroodhouse, Octr the 23rd 1745' over Murray of Broughton's signature. This was addressed to old Lady Cunningham for 'the sum of one hundred pounds sterling, for the use of His Royal Highness, the Prince'.) There was, however, no way back to the good graces of government for Ross Herald who had held centre stage on the never-to-be-forgotten 17th of September. He and the other officers of state who had stood round the Cross that day had been suspended and their pay stopped by order of the Barons of the Exchequer. But by 1749, through the intervention of Lord Lyon Brodie, the suspension was lifted and arrears of pay made over to all but Roderick Chalmers of Portlethen, a resolute Jacobite to the end. Thomas Ruddiman's printer who on Lord Provost Stewart's acquittal published a squib against Hanoverian authority, was severely dealt with, as was one John Finlayson in 1751 for publishing a map of the marches of the erstwhile Highland Army 'and even the secret routs of the Pr . . . ' Episcopalians being inevitably Jacobite, the Scottish Episcopal Church came under the grip of new Penal Laws. Services in their chapel off Carrubber's Close were harshly limited in the size of congregations tolerated. Yet on a personal level more kindly Scotch ways re-asserted themselves. Within four years of Culloden, as Alexander Carlyle recalled, his friend John Home, become the Revd. John Home and minister of Athelstaneford Parish in East Lothian, was living on the friendliest terms with James Hepburn of Keith 'who had been in both the rebellions of 1715 and 1745, and had there been a 3rd ....... would have join'd it also'.

Jacobite sentiment lingered on. But hatred of the Union which had been its powerful ally abated as its benefits accrued for merchants and gentry; though as late as the 1770s young Robert Fergusson was voicing the instinctive feelings of common people as he entertained his Edinburgh tavern cronies with patriotic verse, damning the Union.

Where should this story of the months of Prince Charles Edward's stay at Holyrood have its ending? Perhaps with the dinner to mark the Prince's birthday given in 1787 at a house (it stood until 1909) under the high tenements of St James' Square. The host and hostess were the son-in-law and daughter of Thomas Ruddiman, erstwhile owner and proprietor of the Jacobite *Caledonian Mercury* which had reported the victory at Gladsmuir so glowingly. Robert Burns attended that gathering of elderly Jacobites; the health of the absent Prince was pledged in a bumper, and poet Burns recited verses he had written for the occasion which began 'Afar the illustrious exile roams...'

Or should the ending be the advent of sentimental Jacobitism with the songs of Lady Nairne ('Charlie is my darling' etc etc), herself the grand-daughter of the Laurence Oliphant who had in Edinburgh's High Street somewhat rashly challenged dragoons fleeing from the field of Gladsmuir. Perhaps the last word should be an earlier and fictional one, that of the staunch Edinburgh Whig, Mr Alexander Fairford W.S. of Sir Walter's 'Redgauntlet', who had borne arms for the government side in the 'Forty-Five, and whose attitudes we may be sure were those of many a douce Edinburgh citizen. Fairford, it will be recalled, 'spoke sometimes of the Chevalier, but never either of the Prince, which would have been sacrificing his own principles, or of the Pretender which would have been offensive to those of others'.

In the long perspective of history, the most remarkable aspect of Edinburgh under Jacobite occupation is perhaps the devotion the Bonnie Prince attracted from the ladies. Two-thirds of the ladies of Edinburgh were ardently for the Prince, said Alexander Carlyle. Lord President Duncan Forbes writing after Gladsmuir summed it up:

> All Jacobites, how prudent so ever, became mad, all doubtful people became
> Jacobites, and all bankrupts became heroes, and talked nothing but hereditary

rights and victory; and what was more grievous to men of gallantry, and if you will believe me, much more mischievous to the public, all the fine ladies, if you will except one or two, became passionately fond of the young adventurer, and used all their arts and industry for him, in the most intemperate manner.

But, then, as young Edward Topham of Trinity College, Cambridge would find out to his delight a decade or so later, the flowers of Edinburgh had minds of their own. Perhaps those who so warmed to 'the young Chevalier' instinctively recognised, better than their spouses did, that Scotland needed a royal focus for its loyalties, a focus which the first two Georges so signally failed to give.

But there was something else. Edinburgh *et environs* had learned that Highlanders were human beings after all. In the panic-stricken days of mid-September, stout doors had been put up at the bottom of every important turnpike stair and at the tops and bottoms of closes for protection against marauding Highlanders. These fears had not been realised. Lady Jane Nimmo writing to the ultra-Whig Earl of Marchmont about the invasion of his Redbraes Castle in the Merse of Berwickshire by a detachment from Glengarry's Regiment in the October of 1745 had to concede that they were all remarkably civil, and that the intrusion had ended with her three daughters entertaining the MacDonell officers round a warm fire. Even Patrick Crichton had to modify his view of the 'scurlewheelers' after having had to dine in company which included the two sergeants of the Appin Stewarts who had been assigned to guard Mrs Philp's Greenlaw, and who came with her to Woodhouselie for a visit; he was intrigued by their tales of their adventures. Most remarkable of all had been the insistence of the MacDonalds of Glencoe that they be given the task of guarding against marauders the fine new house by the banks of the Almond of the Earl of Stair, son of the infamous instigator of the Massacre of Glencoe of 1692!

The Commission set up by government in the years after the Forty-five to administer the forfeited estates taken from rebel chiefs were to spawn a succession of enlightened schemes for Highland development. That they were no more successful than many schemes of Highland development of the next 200 years is beside the point. Here in promoting the well-being of the people, rather than merely building military roads and forts, was a new departure in the way Scotsmen looked at the Highlands. The experience of the 'Forty-Five was not all loss.

*His saddlery and ironmongery in the Grassmarket prospering, Patrick Crichton parted with Woodhouselie in 1749 in exchange for Newington House a mile to the south of Edinburgh. But nothing more is known of him though his descendants did well, his grandson, Sir Alexander Crichton, becoming physician to the Russian Czar in the 1820s.*

*Alexander Carlyle was ordained minister of Inveresk Parish, near Musselburgh, in 1748. There he remained until his death in 1805, a champion of the Moderates, a foe to the Evangelicals in the General Assembly of the Church of Scotland, and a luminary of Edinburgh's Age of Enlightenment.*

*After Culloden, Lord Elcho escaped to France. As the years of exile passed and it became ever-clearer that neither King George II nor his successor would grant him a pardon, his animosity towards Charles Edward grew. He died in Switzerland in*

*1787. (It may well be thought that Elcho's fate would have been that of Captain Edward Waverley, had the latter been able to escape the gallows.) Elcho's friend Sir James Steuart, similarly exiled for many years, became the leading political economist in Europe.*

*After Culloden, John Murray of Broughton with Cameron of Lochiel sought to keep the Rising going in the vain expectation of French help. Escaping to the Lowlands he was captured there, but saved his own neck at the expense of Lord Lovat's, by offering himself as King's Evidence at the latter's trial for treason, — for this incurring lasting odium. In 1764 he briefly reappears in Edinburgh's story when the lawyer father of Sir Walter Scott pitched Murray's teacup out of the window of his house in College Wynd after a business visit by the Laird of Broughton.*

*Magdalen Pringle was married to a Berwickshire laird in 1761 but died two years later. One would so much wish to know more of her.*

*John Campbell remained in great reputation as Cashier of the Royal Bank of Scotland until his death in 1777.*

*The Marquis d'Eguilles surrendered after Culloden having pled in vain with the Prince not to risk battle. He returned to France in 1747, and lived to old age, dying in 1784.*

*General Sir John Cope was subjected to a Board of Enquiry for his conduct at Gladsmuir but was acquitted. He died at an advanced age in 1760. Rear-Admiral Byng died famously in front of a firing squad on his own quarter deck eleven years after the 'Forty-Five. Captain Rodney of the Milford went on to fame and fortune. Captain Beavor of the Fox and his entire ship's complement of 160 were lost off Dunbar in the great storm of November 1745 which overwhelmed the frigate.*

*Throughout the barren years that followed his return to France in 1746 Charles Edward never wavered from his ambition to be King. Twenty years after Culloden he was heard to say that 'there is but one thing that I want: all else is brown bread'.*

# Sources

*The Woodhouselie Manuscript;* W & R Chambers, Edinburgh, 1907.

*Anecdotes and Characters of the Times* by the Revd. Alexander Carlyle; Oxford University Press, 1973.

*A Short Account of the Affairs of Scotland in the Years 1744, 1745, 1746* by David, Lord Elcho; Edinburgh, 1907.

*Lord Elcho's Journal* (unpublished).

*A Jacobite Miscellany* (Letters of Magdalen Pringle); ed. Henrietta Taylor; Roxburghe Club, 1948.

*Miscellany of the Scottish History Society;* Edinburgh, 1893. (Diary of John Campbell); also The Diary of John Campbell: a Scottish Banker and the 'Forty-Five (Royal Bank of Scotland), 1995

*Memorials of John Murray of Broughton;* Scottish History Society; Edinburgh, 1898.

*The Book of the Old Edinburgh Club Vol II (Edinburgh at the Time of the Occupation of Prince Charles;* by W.B. Blaikie).

*Minutes of Edinburgh Town Council for 1745;* Vol 65.

*Lochiel of the '45;* by John Sibbald Gibson, Edinburgh University Press, 1994.

*Itinerary of Prince Charles Edward Stuart from his landing in Scotland July 1745 until his departure in September 1746*; Scottish History Society, 1897.

*History of the Rebellion in the year 1745;* by John Home; London 1802.

*Memoirs of the Rebellion in 1745 and 1746;* by the Chevalier de Johnstone; London, 1820.

*Intercepted Post August to December 1745*; ed Donald Nicholas; London, 1956.

*La Mission du Marquis d'Eguilles;* by G Lefèvre-Pontalis; Paris, 1886.

*The Lockhart Papers Vol 2* (Memoirs of the Young Pretender's Expedition in 1745 by a Highland Officer in his Army); London, 1817.

*Narrative of Charles, Prince of Wales' Expedition in Scotland in the year 1745;* by James Maxwell of Kirkconnel; Edinburgh (Maitland Club), 1841.

*History of the Rebellion in the years 1745 and 1746;* Anon (by a contemporary); Roxburghe Club; London, 1944.

*Curiosities of a Scots Charter Chest 1600-1800;* William Brown, Edinburgh 1897.

*The Scots Magazine* for 1745 and 1746.

*The Caledonian Mercury* for 1745.

*Journal of the Heralding Society of Scotland No.7:*

*The Impact of Jacobitism on the Scottish Heralds 1689—1760*; by Malcolm Innes of Edingiht, Lord Lyon of Arms.

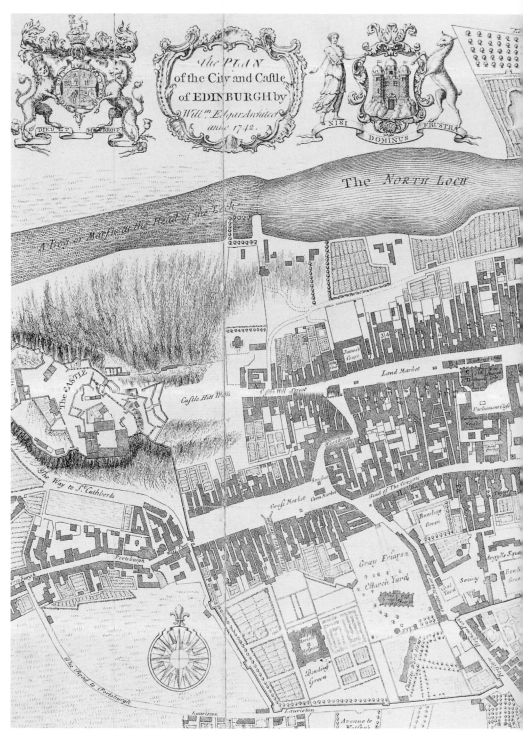

*Edinburgh in 1742 by William Edgar. (excerpt)*

# Some Saltire Publications

| | |
|---|---|
| J D McClure *Why Scots Matters* | 0 85411 039 0 £2.95 |
| Geoffrey Barrow *Robert the Bruce and the Scottish Identity* | 0 85411 027 5 £1.00 |
| I B Cowan Mary Queen of Scots | 0 85411 037 2 £2.50 |
| David Stevenson *The Covenanters* | 0 85411 042 9 £2.95 |
| Kenneth MacKinnon *Gaelic: a Past and Future Prospect* | 0 85411 047 X £7.95 |
| Meston, Sellars and Cooper *The Scottish Legal Tradition* (New Ed) | 0 85411 045 3 £5.99 |
| Rosalind Mitchison (ed.) *Why Scottish History Matters* (contribs from Geoffrey Barrow, A A M Duncan, Alexander Grant, Michael Lynch, David Stevenson, Bruce P Lenman, T M Devine, R H Campbell, Christopher Harvie) | 0 85411 048 8 £5.99 |
| William Neill *Tales frae the Odyssey o Homer owreset intil Scots* | 0 85411 049 6 £7.95 |

### New and Forthcoming Editions:

| | |
|---|---|
| William Ferguson *Scotland's Relations with England : a Survey to 1707* | 0 85411 058 5 £12.99 |
| Paul Scott *Andrew Fletcher and the Treaty of Union* | 0 85411 057 7 £12.99 |
| Paul Scott *Walter Scott and Scotland* | 0 85411 056 9 £7.99 |
| David Stevenson *Highland Warrior: Alasdair MacColla and the Civil Wars* | 0 85411 059 3 £12.99 |
| David Daiches *Robert Burns, the Poet* | 0 85411 060 7 £12.99 |

Thorbjorn Campbell *Standing Witnesses*

Alwyn James *Scottish Roots* (New Edition)

Saltire New Poetry

Raymond Vettese *A Keen New Air*

0 85411 061 5 £15.99

0 85411 066 6 £4.99

0 85411 063 1 £6.99

---

## THE NATION THAT FORGETS ITS PAST IS DEAD

*"The Saltire Society speaks and works for the*
*Scottish people. Its primary concern is the*
*enrichment of life in Scotland."*
**Professor David Daiches,**
**President of the Saltire Society, 1982-86**

The Saltire Society has been active since 1936 in the encouragement of everything that might improve the quality of life in Scotland and restore the country to is proper place as a creative force in European civilisation.

The activities and aims of the Saltire Society are diverse and constantly expanding. They are local as well as national. You will have seen the Society's Housing Design, Civil Engineering and Environmental Planning plaques throughout Scotland The Society's celebrated Award schemes also recognise excellence in many other areas from literature to choral singing. Specific Saltire Awards are sponsored by Commerce and Industry.

*"If more people supported the Society's aims, Scotland would be a better place."*
**Nigel Tranter**

Come and join us, there are many local branches.

Further information from:
The Administrator, The Saltire Society,
9 Fountain Close, 22 High Street,
Edinburgh EH1 1TF.

Telephone: 0131-556 1836